A Stranger in the House

A Stranger in the House

Text by
Robert Hamburger

Photographs by
Susan Fowler-Gallagher

COLLIER BOOKS
A Division of Macmillan Publishing Co., Inc.
New York

Copyright © 1978 by Robert Hamburger

Photographs copyright © 1978
by Susan Fowler-Gallagher

All rights reserved. No part of this book may be reproduced or transmitted in any form or by any means, electronic or mechanical, including photocopying, recording or by any information storage and retrieval system, without permission in writing from the Publisher.

Macmillan Publishing Co., Inc.
866 Third Avenue, New York, N.Y. 10022
Collier Macmillan Canada, Ltd.

Library of Congress Cataloging in Publication Data
Hamburger, Robert, 1943–
A stranger in the house.
1. Afro-American women—Employment—New York (City) 2. Servants—New York (City) 3. New York (City)—Race relations. 4. Women, Black—Employment—New York (City) 5. Social classes—New York (City) I. Fowler-Gallagher, Susan. II. Title.
[F128.9.N4H35   1978b]   331.4'09747'1   78-13015
ISBN 0-02-085370-X pbk.
ISBN 0-02-547610-6

Portions of this work first appeared, in a slightly different form, in the spring 1977 issue of *Southern Exposure*.

First Collier Books Edition 1978

A Stranger in the House is also published
in hardcover by Macmillan Publishing Co., Inc.

Printed in the United States of America

I'll make my report as if I told a story, for I was taught as a child on my homeworld that Truth is a matter of the imagination. The soundest fact may fail or prevail in the style of its telling. . . . If at moments the facts seem to alter with an altered voice, why then you can choose the fact you like best; yet none of them are false, and it is all one story.

> —**Ursula K. LeGuin**
> *The Left Hand of Darkness*

At this hour of the world's history it may be that you, now, have something to learn from us.

> —**James Baldwin**
> "An Open Letter to Mr. Carter,"
> *New York Times*,
> January 23, 1977

Acknowledgments

A BOOK OF THIS SORT IS A COLLABORATIVE EFFORT, AND IT WOULD NOT EXIST IN any form without the trust and participation of the women who shared their narratives with me. This is their book, and I hope they will be proud of it. I also want to thank the employers who welcomed Susan and me into their homes with a minimum of embarrassment and suspicion. It is, after all, an unusual situation to have a writer and a photographer roaming freely around one's home—yet we received cooperation, encouragement, and a few good meals along the way. I would thank the household workers and employers by name, but many of them have asked that I protect their privacy with pseudonyms. Numerous friends have offered me encouragement and criticism, and still others have helped by arranging interviews for me.

During my work on *A Stranger in the House*, I received a big boost from the editors of *Southern Exposure* when they published excerpts from my interviews. And in the spring of 1977 I spent two wonderful months at the MacDowell Colony, where I was able to complete substantial sections of the final text.

Finally, I want to thank two people directly involved in the making of this book: Beth Rashbaum, our editor at Macmillan, for truly caring about our project and for using her own skills to make sure we came out with the book we envisaged; and Susan Fowler-Gallagher for her fine photographs. It was a book we all wanted to do—we worked hard, we shared some adventures, and we learned a great deal from the women whose lives and images make up this book.

—Robert Hamburger

AS IT TAKES FIVE FINGERS ON A HAND TO CAPTURE A PICTURE/MY APPRECIATION goes

Firstly to you/Cynthia Simmons/who from seven on were to be/my closest friend/second mother/thanks for surrounding me with the air from fresh donuts/opera/and endless wisdom/especially the observation that T.V. soap operas are secretly and mysteriously for real/they are/I never/even in my wildest prank/could have been prepared for womanhood without you/your courage wrapped in ironic laughter/is always with me/

Secondly to the other strangers in houses/of this project/who became so much more/even though you travel under pseudonames this book is yours/ your spontaneous cooperation and friendship is here forever recorded/ and you have the heart of my appreciation because you gave me yours/ my camera was just a humble instrument and excuse/for sharing all the hours together/the light in your eyes and the unspoken experience behind your faces touched me/and I hope will reach out to all who take the care and time/to read your words

Thirdly/but not over technically/to my two closest colleagues/Michael Abramson/whose professionalism kept the cameras rolling/the lights flashing/but most of all your unswerving logic kept me going personally/to Peter Crabtree your darkroom humor and know-how helped me inestimably/

Fourthly/to Robert Hamburger/who asked me to join this journey/I accepted and will again/to work with you was an adventure/the feedback/ even though you were halfway around the globe always came at the right time/four A.M. trans-Atlantic into my darkroom/with inspiration you lent me the subtlety to join the personal interview with portrait/thank you for the special energy of collaboration

Lastly and very largely/my appreciation to the families who let me into their homes to witness/to photograph their relationships frankly and honestly/and to the persons behind the scenes at Macmillan/who were the final tender touches in the birthing of this book.

— Susan Fowler-Gallagher

Introduction

A Stranger in the House IS A COLLECTION OF PERSONAL NARRATIVES FROM black women who have been employed in households in the New York area. Although they have household work in common, their experiences in that field have been diverse, and I did not want to deny that variety by manipulating their lives in order to make any particular point. So this book is not about any one thing—it is not a study of race relations, or labor abuses, or immigration, or class and cultural interaction—though it is all these things from time to time.

The diversity of personal experiences creates a diversity of perspectives as well—a colloquium rather than a single statement. Some of these women feel good about their work and good about themselves. They are confident, ambitious, and independent. Others have not quite achieved that degree of autonomy, yet they've found security and comfort—through either their families, close personal ties with their employers, or fervent religious commitment. Almost all these women have had rough times along the way, and though most feel pride in how they've come out, there are one or two women who appear to have been overcome by their burdens. Life has been hard on them, and it remains hard. No one person could possibly embody such a wide range of experiences and attitudes.

In gathering these narratives I interviewed black women almost exclusively. I'm well aware that there are significant numbers of Chicano women doing household work in California and the Southwest; native Hawaiians working in homes of the islands' well-to-do families; orientals working for families on the West Coast; Irish, Scandinavian, and German women working in the Northeast, as well as increasing numbers of Spanish-speaking women from Central and South America. Narratives by women from these various national origins and from assorted areas of America might have given this book the feel of a nationwide survey, but I never intended that kind of thing.

I

In the middle and late 1960s I spent a number of months living in Fayette County, Tennessee—a farming community where the civil rights movement was bitterly, often violently contested. *Our Portion of Hell* (New York: Links Books, 1973) was my attempt to recount the history of this struggle through the assembled voices of the black men and women who experienced it. During our talks, my friends asked all kinds of questions about life in the community where I grew up. Those talks encouraged me to consider doing a book that would be closer to home—a look at racial interaction in the affluent suburban world where I was raised. Soon after that, I unconsciously altered the title of James Baldwin's disturbing essay, "A Stranger in the Village"—and the phrase "a stranger in the house" seemed to pull things together for me by suggesting the extraordinary situation created when a black woman begins work in the home of a well-to-do white family. Certainly, part of my interest in this situation came from the fact that I had been a stranger in the house on my first visit to Tennessee. Except for our shared belief in racial equality, I differed from the Jameson family in almost every imaginable way—race, economic position, cultural experience—all the many distinctions one can find between the life of a black farmer in the South and that of a white graduate student from New York. Yet we bridged that vast gap to form a valued and continuing friendship. When a black woman leaves the rural South to enter a white household in the urban or suburban North, she too begins as a stranger in the house. But whereas I arrived as a volunteer civil rights worker, as a respected guest, these women enter a new and unfamiliar space as paid employees—and there is a world of difference between the two situations. Even so, virtually all things remain possible: personal growth and enrichment, economic exploitation, becoming "one of the family," painful anxiety, even direct physical confrontation. How black women have met the challenges and opportunities of this situation is the subject of this book.

Working on this book brought me back to communities like the one in which I was raised, and to memories of my childhood contact with our household help. There were household workers as far back as I can remember, not simply in our home, but in almost every home I entered. I remember some names—Mary, Annie, Vasena, Noel, Betty, Louise—but very little about the lives of these women. I remember liking all the women who lived with us, accepting them as transient members of our family—and yet it seems incredible to me now that I showed little curiosity in their dark skin, where they came from, what their families were like, or how they spent their free time. It puzzled me that some of these women were married, yet only saw their husbands and children on their days off, and perhaps not even then. But seen through the eyes of a child, these women almost always appeared in good spirits.

There was little haughtiness and lots of apparent good will in our family's relations with the women who worked for us. When the door from the kitchen swung open and our maid began serving dinner, someone was bound to say something to bring her into the conversation. Later, if I wanted a second helping of something, my mother would ring a little dinner bell and then hurriedly prompt me, "Be sure you tell her how much you liked it." I don't think the household work itself was particularly difficult, but the hours were long, very long—from seven, when my father came down for coffee, until eight at night when the dinner dishes were cleaned and put away. The women who worked for us ate alone in the kitchen, and when they were done with work, they went off to their bedroom to watch television.

At Christmas there were always *lots* of presents for our maid. My mother would do all the shopping and then have each of us fill out one or two cards. A handbag, a sweater, a nightgown, a bracelet, some money; it seems now as if the same boxes were opened year after year, the same exclamations of joy heard—but no kisses exchanged, no hugs, no touching.

Over the years, the women who passed through our home became part of our family history, but they were largely excluded from family activities. I have no clear memory of ever riding in a car with any of these women except to take them to and from the station on their days off. I don't even have a clear memory of seeing any of them outdoors. Serving meals, bustling about in the kitchen, doing laundry in the basement, moving from room to room doing light cleaning, serving hors d'oeuvres in the den at parties and family gatherings—these are the places and activities I associate with them. These memories are affectionate but vague—names and faces that were close to us yet always just outside the family circle. Their presence in our home never opened into fuller, more complex encounters. A large part of the personal impulse behind this book was to return to this extraordinary meeting of strangers, this time seeing it through the eyes of the working women themselves. I call this extraordinary because, with the exception of institutional environments such as the armed services and prisons, there are no situations outside the South where blacks and whites are placed in such intimate daily contact with one another.

II

One experience that all the women in this book share is immigration and the challenges of adjusting to a new environment. This movement of black people from the rural South to urban centers in the North is the central fact in any historical account of black household workers. When Reconstruction ended in 1877, Jim Crow laws were passed throughout the South, and the paternalistic mood of race relations was replaced by increasing violence and terror. The North appeared to offer blacks something different—the promise of greater racial tolerance, growing industry that spawned peripheral jobs which unskilled black workers might win if they were lucky, and a growing middle class that demanded a large influx of unskilled poor suited for domestic service. As a result, disenchanted young blacks began heading North in the 1880s.

By 1910 there were 415,533 southern-born blacks in the North, and by

1920 there were 737,423. During this wave of immigration, black women came in greater numbers than black men—5 women for every 4 men.[1] The vast majority of women who found employment were hired as household workers. Before 1915 almost 80 percent of black working women in the North were involved in domestic service. Many of these women had been persuaded to come North by a network of employment agents who traveled through the South offering prospective black immigrants transportation and a guaranteed job on their arrival in northern cities. Naïve young black women became, in effect, indentured servants by accepting terms of service that gave them "Justice's Tickets" to the North. Once these women were signed up, they filed aboard steamships that carried them up the Atlantic coast, segregated uncomfortably in steerage quarters along with luggage and white passengers' pets. By 1910 New York had the highest statewide percentage of working black women outside the South. The message to black women was clear: if you want to work, and if you're sick of rural life and the servitude of tenant farming, come North and become a household worker. To move suddenly from a sharecropper's cabin in the rural South to the home of an affluent white family in a northern city was an enormous challenge, but tens of thousands of southern black women did exactly that.

There is no question that these black women were the most marginal group in America's labor force. Some black women found jobs in manufacturing and mechanical industries during World War I, but the pithy observation "Last hired; first fired" has surely been borne out by the history of black working women. With the exception of farm labor, household work remained the main vocational opportunity for black women until World War II. Only then did they begin to penetrate the industrial labor market and professional areas in significant numbers. As a result, the percentage of black women employed as domestic workers has declined steadily over the years, but the greatest changes did not happen until relatively recently. Up to 1965 there were still close to 1 million black household workers—about one third of all black working women. From 1965 to 1974 a dramatic change took place that saw close to a half million black women leave their jobs as household workers. The Johnson administration's War on Poverty contributed to this change by helping move black women into clerical and professional jobs from which they had previously been excluded owing to racial discrimination and lack of training. Also, young women who grew up during the years of civil rights protest often loathed the whole idea of domestic service and refused to consider it as an acceptable way to earn a living. Because of this, there

---

[1] All statistical information here comes from materials assembled by the Bureau of Census. *Negro Population in the United States, 1790–1915* and *Negroes in the United States, 1920–1932* are both valuable sources.

have not been enough native American household workers to meet demands in recent years. Employers and agencies have had to recruit workers from Puerto Rico, Jamaica, and other nations in the Caribbean. It is not uncommon for employers to go to some trouble to recruit an illegal alien and then pay particularly low wages, allowing fear of deportation to muffle any complaints.

The narratives of the women in this book recapitulate the outlines of this historical summary in terms of personal experience. Also, these real experiences ought to reveal the inadequacy of the images our culture has created to define black household workers. Aunt Jemima, *Gone With the Wind, Imitation of Life*, Faulkner's Dilsey, even our more open-minded situation comedies, have brought us back repeatedly to a small cluster of clichés that dull our moral imagination when we begin to accept them as accurate depictions of reality. A few employers seemed astonished, even amused, that I wanted to talk with their help for a few hours, and one woman actually told me that she didn't think her maid had more than ten minutes' worth of information that would interest me. Out of a whole life, not more than ten minutes' worth sharing with another person! An employer like this is surely dealing with a preconceived image rather than with the woman who lives in her house. No other employer I met said anything as outrageous as this, and yet one of the frequent demands made by women in this book is that they be treated like human beings—not like machines, not like dogs, not like servants, but like *human beings*. Surely something is amiss when this complaint is voiced repeatedly. And something is surely wrong when, after a two-hour interview, a household worker can say to me, "You know, you know more about me than Mr. and Mrs. W——, and I've been with them for two years."

It is obvious that I believe curiosity, communication, and simple fairness to be useful antidotes to the snobbery that has sometimes characterized the treatment of household workers, but no working person in America should have to depend upon individual gestures of decency for his health and security. Household workers still lack most of the specific legal guarantees that working people in most other occupations already take for granted: clearly specified contractual obligations concerning work hours, work obligations, sick leave, paid vacation, overtime, health and hospital insurance, and strictly enforced social security payments. One reason for this is that "domestic servants" are explicitly excluded from the National Labor Relations Act of 1935 and its subsequent amendments. In other words, the United States government refuses to guarantee legal collective bargaining rights for household workers.[2] To be sure, some women have been gener-

---

[2] The constitutionality of the National Labor Relations Act rests upon the federal government's power to regulate interstate commerce. Because it is difficult to imagine

ously provided for; there are instances where employers have backed up their affection and gratitude by taking it upon themselves to guarantee these work benefits. But hard-working people should not have to hope for good will to deliver these necessities. Criticizing stingy employers is not the solution; it is the responsibility of state and federal legislatures to frame laws that will bring household work into the mainstream of American labor.

III

I want to say something now about the format I've chosen and about oral history as a literary genre. To begin with, I want to acknowledge the great debt my work owes to that of Oscar Lewis and Robert Coles. This book is not modeled on either man's work, but the presence of their books offered me valuable support at various stages in the preparation of my own work. In his introduction to *The Children of Sanchez* and in his remarkable books, Lewis confirmed my feeling that serious documentary work can offer the pleasure and complexity of literature. And when I felt uncomfortable, even hypocritical, in the role of invisible historian, when I decided to briefly introduce my thoughts and feelings among the personal narratives that make up the body of this book, it was good to know that Dr. Coles had made a similar commitment in his "Children of Crisis" series.

We imagine our oral historian to be objective yet sympathetic, directive but nonmanipulative—but we do not really know, because typically, the historian removes himself from his text, leaving us with a kind of *persona in absentia*. This kind of illusion may be useful in many works, but once I've raised the issue of how white people interact with black household workers, a serious reader ought to be curious, perhaps even insistent, to have some indication of how I responded during the interviews which brought me in contact with these women. Simply to record my voice as interviewer would not really indicate the spirit of the exchange that went

---

how household work affects interstate or foreign commerce, the drafters of the NLRA must have excluded household workers from their legislation in order to protect the consistency of their constitutional argument. As a result, under Findings and Policy, section 2, part 3, we find:

> The term "employee" shall . . . not include any individual employed as an agricultural laborer, or in domestic service of any family or person at his home, or an individual employed by his parent or spouse . . .

Whatever the compelling legal arguments might have been, the simple fact remains that the NLRA guaranteed the right of self-organization and collective bargaining to just about everyone, but it excluded farm workers, household workers, and children working for their parents. No matter how hard they work, no matter what economic abuses they suffer at their jobs, these people are not "employees" under this landmark of labor legislation.

on, and it would surely distract readers from the movement of these women's lives. I have chosen instead to write short prefaces to the narratives. In these notes I have tried to avoid excessive interpretation or any other excesses that might divert too much attention from the narratives themselves. Often I simply suggested the mood of the interview—its setting, or perhaps some moment that stayed with me. These prefaces were not written as paradigms of right thinking, but rather as evidence that I was there, taking part in a complex and ambiguous process—speaking with strangers.

To tell one's story, one's true story, is finally an act of imagination. These narratives are autobiographical improvisations—people gathering their lives together on the spot with no real chance to return to their words and exert a writer's prerogative of revision. What structure there is comes from my simple strategy of encouraging these women to recount their experiences chronologically. The accounts have been edited, but not, I hope, in a way that intrudes on the narrator's voice, or on her feelings about herself and the world she encounters. By agreeing to talk with me, these women became artists of a sort—selecting materials consciously and unconsciously; choosing words, memories, and associations; compressing the years of their lives into a narrative representation of who they are. Oscar Lewis put it well, I think, in his introduction to *The Children of Sanchez:*

> If one agrees with Henry James that life is all inclusion and confusion while art is all discrimination and selection, then these life stories have something of both art and life.[3]

There is no way to verify the factual matter in these histories, nor is that of overriding importance in a work like this. I assume that all the women told me the truth as they understood it, but all autobiographies are dialogues between the events of the past and the life we give them in the present, between who we were and who we are, between the external world and those habits of mind that modify reality in the very process of perception and reflection. Memory does not reproduce the past, it recreates it. All this happens as part of the process of narration, and, because of this, I think an attentive reader will find in these histories not only useful information and ideas, but also the challenges and rewards of literature.[4]

---

[3] Oscar Lewis, *The Children of Sanchez* (New York: Random House, Vintage, 1961), p. xxi.

[4] Indeed, the question of what happens when a lower-class servant enters the household of a well-to-do family has preoccupied novelists since the origin of the novel and has provided our literature with some of its most enduring heroines—Pamela, Moll Flanders, Becky Sharp, and Jane Eyre to name just a few. The most convincing

In the final paragraph of "Manners, Morals, and the Novel," Lionel Trilling explains the moral usefulness of the novel:

> . . . Its greatness and its practical usefulness lay in its unremitting work of involving the reader himself in the moral life, inviting him to put his own motives under examination, suggesting that reality is not as his conventional education has led him to see it. It taught us, as no other genre ever did, the extent of human variety and the value of this variety. It was the literary form to which the emotions of understanding and forgiveness were indigenous, as if by the definition of the form itself.[5]

I think that oral history in general and these personal narratives in particular will engage readers in a similar way. There is great human variety in these accounts and the moral challenge of an extraordinary social encounter. It's up to you now, as readers, to join the colloquium, to listen attentively, and to answer.

---

explanation for this phenomenon is given in Lionel Trilling's fine essay, "Manners, Morals, and the Novel" (*The Liberal Imagination: Essays on Literature and Society* [New York: Doubleday, 1953], p. 201). "All literature," he insists, "tends to be concerned with the question of reality," and nowhere are our ideas of reality put to a greater test than in the uncertain encounter between social classes. And it is this encounter that often marks a turning point in the lives of the household workers I spoke with.

[5] Ibid., p. 215.

A Stranger in the House

Elizabeth Knox

A DRIZZLING NIGHT ON WYKOFF STREET IN BROOKLYN. LIZZIE KNOX IS DRESSED all in white, stooped over from arthritis. Her apartment is tidy, in perfect order—aging furniture with a few good years left. Her church gave a "This Is Your Life" evening for her on Sunday, and some unopened presents lay stacked in a corner. Hanging on the back of her bedroom door is the tangerine-colored gown she wore to the church testimonial. She beams delightedly as she holds it up for me to see. "I want you to tell Bobby about all this," she says. Bobby is my dear friend—he's often told me Lizzie is his second mother. She joined his family when his mother was pregnant with him, and she stayed with them through his childhood and years of college. When I sit down to speak with Lizzie, I notice framed photographs of Bobby and his brother Howard on the end table. As we talk, various members of Lizzie's family pop in and out on assorted errands—and before we've finished, I've had a chance to meet her two grandchildren, Bobby and Howard, named after the two white boys she loved so dearly.

When the interview is over and I'm on my way out, I extend my hand to say goodbye. Lizzie reaches out and pulls me to her in a warm hug. "I'm just gonna do this," she says as she plants a kiss on my cheek.

*M*y name is Elizabeth Knox, and I was born in Camden, South Carolina, 802 Market Street, in 1903. I'm seventy-four. I had a beautiful childhood. If you ever go to Camden and go to the hospital to look around you'll see big trees—I imagine they so big, huge now—well, my grandfather planted those trees. My grandfather remembered slavery—he was too young to do anything then but carry the mail. He told me he found some money one time and bought some bread and buried it in a hole. He was afraid to let anybody know. And when he would pass by each day, he would dig out the hole and eat some of the bread. When slavery ended he used to drive a carriage for the wealthy ladies in Camden. He did that quite a few years.

You know, I appreciate it all so much more now, because I've seen so many things happen—and I just love to tell people what a nice, beautiful childhood I had. I had a lot of love, and they always dressed me up so nice—me and my brother Dave. My father had a restaurant, and sometimes he'd sell ice cream from a cart. I remember he'd sing:

> Hokey pokey ice cubes,
> Ice cream blocks
> Just fine!
> Just fine!

Somethin like that. He would be out on the corner and give me an ice cream, and the children would look, you know.

You know Larry Doby, the baseball player? He's from Camden. Well, he was interviewed on WMCA, and he said he explained to his son that it wasn't the way people say it was with blacks and whites in the South. Not in Camden—they got along. Our family lived on Savage Avenue, and we associated with the white people that lived on our street. As you go further up the street, there was families that had somebody do their work for them, but round about where we lived there was white families—I shouldn't say they were poor, because they all had somethin, but they weren't wealthy like the families down the street—and we all were friends. My mother would go to their house and have coffee, and they could come to her house and visit. That's the way it was.

Durin the first war we would go out and pick cotton and stay the whole week. The war—oh, now it brings back memories. It was sad because when the soldiers was called to service they'd have a big thing at the church for them, and the preacher would preach, and they would sing, and I remember the girls cryin about their boyfriends. Oh, it was so sad! I didn't have a boyfriend to go in the army. I was only fifteen, and my boyfriend was young like me—he was a nice little fellow. But then I married at sixteen—the war was over, and I married a soldier. I met him one day at his aunt's—the same woman who lived next door to us. He'd been in the service and experienced everything, and he sat down with this little boy I was datin and said, "Do you know Lizzie Knox?"

So this boy said, "Yes, that's my girlfriend."

And the soldier said, "I'm gonna marry her!" Just like that.

The poor boy came down to me, and he was cryin, and he told me what John had said. I said, "No, I don't like him."

But he worked on it, and we got married. That poor little boy—he was so nice. I just wanted to be happy because my childhood was so beautiful. I just wanted that to continue. Even after my father died, we was still with my grandparents. I think that's why it was so nice—bein with them. If you could've spoken to my mother, she would've said, "Elizabeth's a nice girl, a quiet girl. Girls'll be walkin round with their boyfriends, and she'll be out on the porch readin." I was inclined to do that until this fellow came along. We didn't move far away—I was just right around the corner, near my mother. I didn't work; he didn't let me work. That was the trouble.

I just stayed around, and, of course, when Mildred was born I took care of her. And after that, Louise Virginia was born. She died five years ago.

In 1932 we left Camden and went to work with Dr. and Mrs. McCone in Sumpter. We lived in a three-room house in the back that the cook lived in before. And then I worked some, because my husband had no excuse. He was the kind of jealous type, and he kept tellin me I wasn't leavin home to work. But there, it was no distance to the McCones' house—all I had to do was walk over there—and I'd still be close to home. I worked before I was married—takin care of children and helpin my mother do laundry on Fair Street after my father died—and I wanted to work again. Oh, I enjoyed when we lived with the McCones. If you could speak to my daughter, she would tell you. When we lived there we was really happy. Of course, there was only white children in the neighborhood, but my daughter used to play with them. I remember they had a fight once, and her father said, "All right, if anybody hits you, you hit back." So that's what she would do. The next time she had a fight, a couple of parents came back to tell the father and me. But their kids had hit first. That's one thing—if they would start the fight, you hit them.

I said before, my husband was the jealous type—very jealous. Well, our marriage didn't turn out so nice, cause he was too jealous. He got angry sometimes—he was so foolish. He could make your life miserable, very miserable. So I said, "Well now, I can't take this anymore." So I left him and left the South. Louise would say, "Momma, I wish you would go away, because Daddy does this and that to you." I decided that I should just not take this from him, that life was no good—so I left. I'll tell you what happened. The McCones were movin North, so they said, "If you wanna go, we'll take you." So I sent the children to stay with my mother, and I hid my clothes under the doorstep. I got up the next mornin, put my clothes in the car, and just left.

They found a house in Larchmont. Just beautiful! And this is funny—it was my day off, and when I looked outside, there was my husband standin up there in front of the door. He got my address somehow, and he was so happy to see me. He took me on where he was livin—but he had it in him—he hit me. I got homesick—I wanted to see my children. And I'd come North to get away from my husband, and now I was livin with him. But then my husband got sick, really sick. He didn't eat a thing. Then I said, "All right, I'm goin to take you home." And I'm tellin you—when he got on that bus and we were goin home, he started eatin. He didn't have any money, and I had my money saved in my shoe—well, he didn't stop eatin, and I kept takin my shoe off the whole ride home.

I was so glad to *be home*! My God—I really was! But he couldn't live with us—he was just so jealous. My sister would have boyfriends comin in, and he would say, "Oh, they're comin to see you!" And I shouldn't tell you this—to go over it again—he would get under the house and listen to everything we talked about. Then he would say to us, "I heard everything you said." Isn't that awful? *Isn't it?* Oh, my goodness!

Then I got a job—I always wanted to work. There was a married couple with a new baby, and I would go take care of their place till the baby got a bit older. But you know my husband would meet me there. He was really somethin. I was goin to work, and he got near the hedge—and he'd jump up and frighten me so. He'd say, "Ahah! I gotchya now." Nobody around, nobody near—but he didn't hit me, he walked on with me to this job and kept an eye on me. Then I got another job, but he didn't bother me there to much—he stopped gettin behind trees and everything. Then my cousin sent for me. He worked for millionaires in Richmond, and he got me this job across the road from his. So here I am with the beautiful uniform, a gray dress for evening and a white dress for anywhere in town. I stayed there four weeks, and I was so homesick! I told my cousin I was goin home. He said, "Well, I wish you'd wait until Joe comes back."

I said, "No, nothin doin. I wanta go now, cause if he comes back he won't allow me to leave."

So I left. The first time I've ever been homesick. The houses were so— they had to be far apart because they were estates. It was nice for somebody who would want to stay there, but, oh, I couldn't stand it. Here I am, just this one house way away from everything, and they would be gone, and it was so lonely. And the sun would set right on the kitchen window, and you could see the big sunset—oh, I was just so homesick! It was beautiful, but I was just homesick. So I went home again.

When I went home, my sister wanted me to come to Brooklyn and bring her little girl. I never wanted to live in Brooklyn somehow. I heard it wasn't a nice place to live.

So she said, "Oh come and bring Mickey for me."

She kept writin me and writin me, so I said, "All right, I'll come," and started out. I left on Monday—never liked leavin home on the weekend—and got there Tuesday May 18, 1939—I remember.

My sister got me a job with the Elmans, and I stayed there thirty years. All the families I've worked for were nice but the Elmans are different—they just are different. Thirty years I stayed with the family—it was like home to me. Mrs. Elman, she was just—oh, I wish you could have known her! Mr. Elman was a furrier. They were so nice. Their oldest daughter was still living there with her husband—Mr. and Mrs. Millman—and she was pregnant with her first child. Harriet, the younger daughter, was in Brooklyn College. When I started work, Mrs. Elman had just lost a son—Barney. Somthin was wrong with him—I can't remember—but he died two weeks before. And there was Allie—he was in medicine school at the time, and they didn't let him know that his brother had died, because you have the exams then, you know. The family were always so nice to me—I always felt at ease with everybody.

The memories is so beautiful, so beautiful! On Fridays Mrs. Elman would cook. We'd have thirteen, fourteen at the table sometimes. It was beautiful on Friday night. I would put dinner on the table and she would fix the plates. Then I'd get the dessert ready and take that in. I knew if it was meat, they'd have tea; if it was a dairy meal, then they'd have coffee. I just loved it—I loved her. When I was sick, she would tell me to lay down or take somethin to taste—and I can still hear her—"Elizabeth, you are so stubborn! So stubborn!" It was just so nice as the years went by.

Bobby was born August 25, 1939—I remember everyone's birthday. He was my baby—I took care of him—my baby. I mean, they didn't just leave him there—Mrs. Millman was there, but then she would go out to the store so her husband could do defense work. By then they had moved out from Mrs. Elman, but I would take care of Bobby when they needed me. I sent Bobby to school the first day—we always discussed this. Mrs. Millman said, "A mother wanta send her child to school for the first day, they wanta remember that." But *I* sent him to school. *I* did. I went out the door to see that he got on the bus—he hugged me and said goodbye and all. He called me "Itty." The family called me "Elizabeth," but when Bobby came along he couldn't say "Elizabeth," only "Itty." And after "Itty," it was "Lizzie."

Bobby knew I just had to be a member of the family, because here I was, all the time. He knew I was somethin to him, so one day he said, "You my cousin!"

I said, "No."

"You my aunt!"

I said, "No, I'm Lizzie and I love you." I was there when he was born, so he never asked where I came from. Far back as he could remember—there I was.

He would help me clean—and he was so little. I would tie a kerchief on my head—you seen people do that—so he'd say, "I want one!" I'd tie his head up with a white cloth, and he would take the dust rag and *help* me. He would dust—oh, he would look up at me and—imagine him with his head tied up! Oh yes! He was a good boy with me. I never spanked him, never had to spank him. When I said, "Do this!" he'd do it, or, "Don't do that," he wouldn't. But to his grandmother and mother, he wasn't like that.

I remember we went to cousin Norman's wedding. That was some wedding! After the wedding we went to Coney Island. Bobby must have been six or seven, and he wanted to get on all the rides. He went and got on the loop-the-loop—and he was frightened, lookin so afraid. Every time he got where I was standin, he held his head. He wanted to get out, but they didn't stop. Just when he was about to enjoy the ride, it was all over and he had to get out. He was a sweet little boy.

My mother and Mildred came to Brooklyn, and Mildred got a job. Sometimes she'd come out to the Elmans' house and stay overnight. Everyone became so fond of Mildred—they liked her so much. So Mildred—when her first son was born, she said, "I'm gonna name him Robert." Then Howard—that's Bobby's younger brother—said, "You got a Bobby; when you have the next one, name him Howard." Nine years later she had another boy and named him Howard.

My husband was still in Camden aggravatin my family, but he died when his oldest grandson was only about two months old. Howard's like his grandfather—he's a musician, plays with the band. He's always happy to hear how his grandfather could play. My husband could play anything—any instrument he picked up. Well, he died, and after my mother left Camden, I had no one there. I stopped goin back years ago.

I'd buy the Millman boys toys every birthday—whatever I could find, until they grew up and went to college. I didn't know what to buy them, so I gave them money when they got too big for toys. One day Howard said to me, "Why do you give me your money? I don't need it. Don't give me your money." I don't know—I guess he didn't want to take my money anymore; he got too big. Bobby never said that though. I gave him money until he was really grown up. The thing about it—he appreciated it so; he cherished all of that. He says such nice things to me when we talk on the phone. He loves me, he really does. And what I did for him—I got a lot of pleasure out of it, cause he was such a good boy.

After I stopped working, I used to go to the store, and Mr. Millman would go buy lunch and we'd all talk. Now he's sold the store, but we call and talk to each other and keep in touch that way. Bobby still comes to see me once or twice a year. Such nice people, so many nice times to remember. Those years with Mrs. Elman—they used the kitchen for everything, and we would all sit at the table together and eat. We were always together, all the way. We shared our joys, and we shared our sorrows—that's what I always say to them. It was just nice. Beautiful.

I had to stop work cause of arthritis. My knees swelled and got stiff. Painful! Dear, it was so painful! So finally I had to stop workin. I retired, and after that I got social security cause Mr. Millman had been payin it for me. Then I went to Welfare, and I've been gettin disability ever since. But I had to become adjusted you know. It was hard at first to stay home. That was the hard part of it—but my knee was so painful and stiff, I couldn't move. It's not that way anymore. I been goin out to the Center every day since the first of April. The Center's right across the street. Isn't that nice? A few years ago my pastor said, "Go around to the Center. Some of you are senior citizens." And I been goin ever since. I used to give my time in the kitchen; now I'm helpin em at lunch.

My grandchildren are doin fine, growin nicely. Bobby, he's not as smart as Howard, but he could be. They're both in school. Howard went to PS Fifty-one, where you skip a grade. That was a beautiful time in his life, and mine too. I would go to the school, and it was a joy to go and watch them dance—they had such talent down there.

Last week my church gave me a "This Is Your Life" party. They told me they were goin to do it, but I didn't want it. It required a lot of doin and gettin the family together—I just felt that I didn't want to bother.

Then they talked to my daughter, and she worked on it. And the evenin was beautiful! Mario Larolla went. He's my landlord, sort of, but I introduced him as my son. He called me "Nana" too—all of em do. This is something beautiful too—they say they love me. Eleanor, she don't go to work until she ring my bell and tell me she's goin out. I'm lucky to have them in the house. When I got up to speak, I just said what I felt. They came in so fast—my family, my friends—I didn't see who was sittin there. So then I asked them to stand up, and they stood up. And yeah, oh boy, I was really dressed up—my daughter had seen to that. And I was proud; I've had a nice life—I told em that.

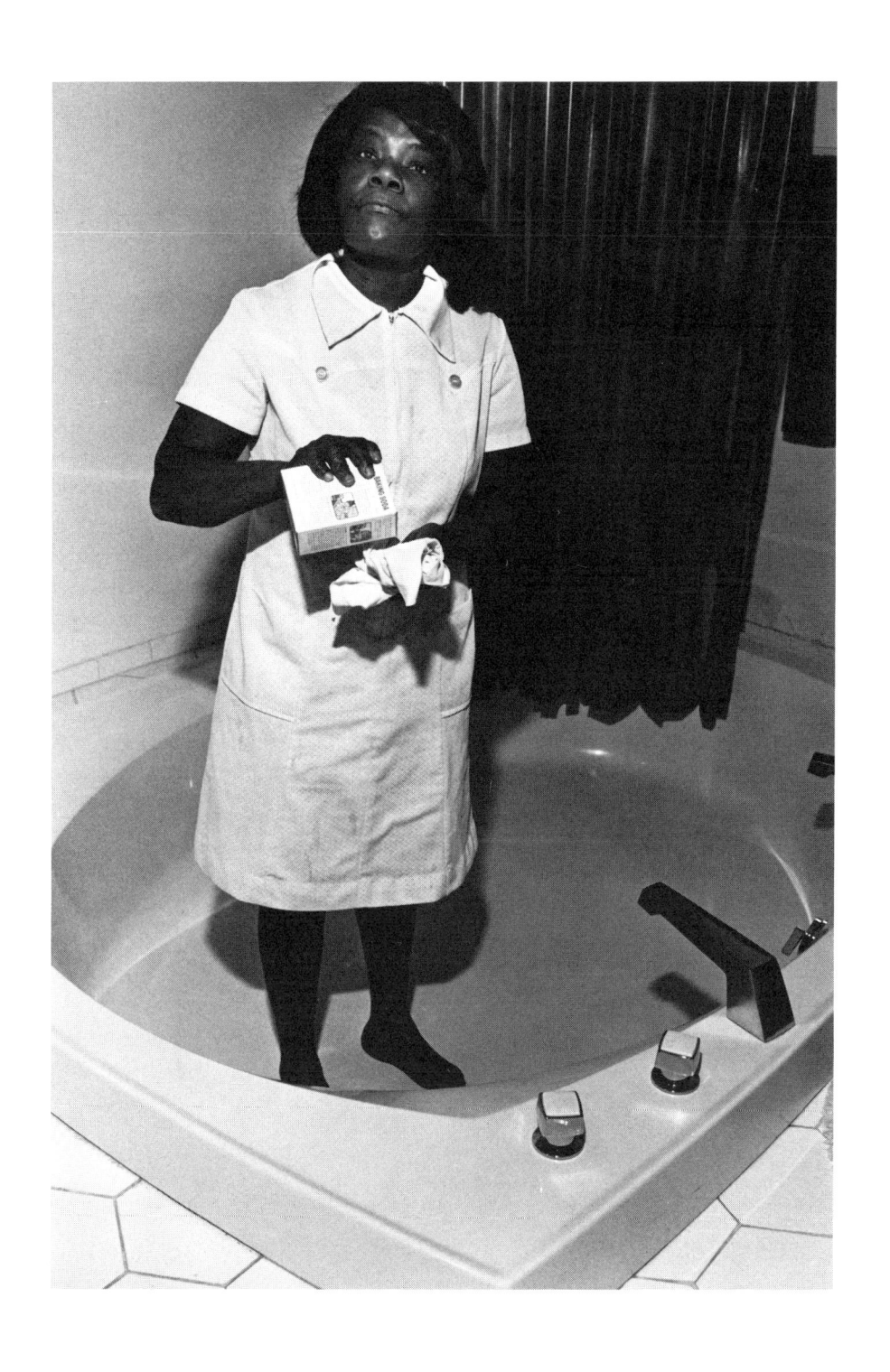

Ellen O'Hara

I HAVE TWO GENERAL STRATEGIES IN MY INTERVIEWS—ONE IS TO ASK QUESTIONS that will help the speaker trace the movement of her life from childhood up to the present; the other is to select crucial moments in the narrative at which to press the speaker for specific details and extended reflection. But with Ellen O'Hara my procedures seemed to run aground. Ellen seemed comfortable speaking within the framework of her life history, but I often felt thwarted in my attempts to get her to respond analytically to her experience or to fill in her account with descriptive elements. Again and again, I would prod her for minute particulars that might help establish time and place, her economic circumstances, her feelings—but I rarely succeeded. Ellen's discussion invariably returned to passages from the Bible which she kept by her side throughout the interview. It is her most treasured possession, full of handwritten marginal notes and strips of torn paper poking out to mark her favorite verses.

Now I understand that Ellen did not resist my questions—she simply does not see the world in the terms I encouraged her to use. It was not Ellen who held out stubbornly—I created my own frustration by persisting in trying to draw from her the kind of material I had decided a good interview should have. This became increasingly clear as I transcribed her words. Ellen was simply being herself, just as I had encouraged her to be before we began the interview. When she "digressed" from her narrative to introduce biblical passages, I would do my best to listen patiently and then to nudge her gently back to the story. But now it seems quite wrong to call such moments "digressions." What was she digressing from? If I found it difficult to keep Ellen's narrative moving through a world of places and objects and money and personal relationships, it is because these aspects of experience are relatively insignificant compared to her relation to God. It is as if the world in which we work and live and leave traces of ourselves among the many lives we touch—all that seems a kind of illusion to Ellen—whereas the changeless visions of the biblical prophets and the teachings of Jesus represent the *real* world, a perfect interior world, that brings her peace and stirs her to sing for joy. "I always speak to God first," she says. A simple principle, the basis of all religion, but I've met few people who live as closely to their faith as Ellen.

My name is Ellen O'Hara. I'm forty-eight and I was born in the country, in St. Thomas, brought up in St. Michaels with my father. He was a shopkeeper—it seemed he sold everything, everything. From my remembrance my father had three shops—two small ones that he had owned and a big one that he had rented—a liquor shop. He used to sell chicken parts, rice, flour, sugar, lead pencils, and exercise books. My father was a real intelligent man. He raised pigs, goats, chickens. I was happy there.

It was fun as a child. We used to run around, or play ball, rounders—you throw up the ball and catch it, about six of us together, and we go away around. And I had loved cricket. We had a big team from Barbados—Australia goin to Barbados, English people too to Barbados, Trinidad people, and Jamaica people. The majority of the people around me were black, but still, we have whites too, we always see white people all around. They had a plantation on a hill called Wallace Plantation, and the white boys and girls, the very rich people, they go to school in a buggy. But we play together, the black and the white, ride horseback and donkey. We had, you know, a kind of unity. We accustomed to one another.

Really, for my growin up I was very happy. I can remember I used to walk about and collect children and carry them to Sunday school. And two white people used to teach me a kind of embroidery in a sewing club. Miss Agnes—there was very good people used to take care of the blacks. They was Christians. For the poor children they ran, they called it "the barefoot Sunday school." Those that didn't have anyone to help them—these two white people would take these kids, collect them, take them and teach them. I used to go to both services—they had one dress and one barefoot. One used to be at two o'clock and the other used to be at three. We used to have prayin and fastin—so I came up very religious. My uncle was a minister. He used to play the organ for the Moravian Church. I used to sing for two choirs.

I liked the ministry. I loved singing in the choir—I grew up in those two choirs. We used to have to wear white—covered our head, at that time we could not go up on the rostrum bare heads. I was ready to go anywhere in the ministry—I loved the ministry. People think that ministry means just goin to the church and preach, but ministry means "servant," the servant of God. So if you're a servant of God, you should be able to help everyone—not because you are white and I am black. I love everyone, in sickness and everything.

The first work I do is for Jewish people at the shirt factory. To tell you the truth I like any work that I can do. I want to do something to help myself. At that time we used to make ten or twelve shirts a day. A man used to cut the cloth by machine; we had a collar-maker, someone to put on the pockets, and we had girls that used to sew on the buttonholes. So

I only put together the shirt. You have to carry your own machine. Only black people at the machines, but the Jewish people were there to supervise, and we all got along very good. The black honored the white. I think that you should be respectable to everybody, and I respect the smallest child. I think you should be always humble. And the Bible say to honor those who have authority over you. The Bible speak about masters and mistress—"Be subject to your masters." Servants be subject to your masters, and your masters be subject to you. You see, if people would live accordin to the Word, we would live. The world want a revival, that is, to my knowledge the world want a revival—a revival of that love which begat love. If we had love for each other it would be different.

When I worked for the Jewish people at the factory I met my husband. Not that he worked there—he was a cabinet-maker. He had a good brain. We had four children—Eustace, Coral, Charles, and Michael—three boys and one girl. Coral, that's the girl. Have a pretty name. She's pretty, too—

like him, kind of higher brown, pinker. I am dark, but she's the only one that take after him. She is nice. She's a teacher. She went to a college and she graduate. When my husband died, the first child was eight, Coral was seven—I got her quick behind him—Charles was five, and Michael was only fifteen months old. So I educate the children myself without any father. It was not easy, you know. So you understand how hard I had it. I had to do actually two and three jobs. I had to pray and fast—that is what helped me along, the prayer and fasting. Some days we go to church five o'clock mornins, and you stay a day. The people group together— we go through the night until morning, without anything, without water. That is where I got my strength. Nobody has never invite me—just the spirit of God lead me there. All my children still keep in church except the biggest one. The first boy is not so good. He become as—he say that it is good to live like a bird. He mean he always fly, always out. He don't stay. I tell him that is not good. The old people used to say, "A black sheep!" Some people say, "A prodigal son," but I don't know what he is. But I know that God is able to change him. He like the company that is not good, and he don't like workin, and that is very wicked. I have to work. I always loved workin from the time I come up.

My husband died eighteen years ago. He died sudden. He worked the day, and lie down the night and died. And after he died I take up housekeeping. In Barbados they carry two or three people in the home. You have a cook and some person to take care of the children—in some homes that can afford it, not all. The poorer class people have one.

I was with a family in Barbados six years, to keep the children, you know. I lived with them, and on the whole, I loved housekeeping. I had feel all right because me and the lady used to get along good. What used to draw her to me is the singin—she used to love to hear me sing. She say that used to do something for her. Even if I am out in the yard—the husband used to keep his gamecocks, so I really used to love to go out there to feed em, singin all the while. She would come outside and she hear me singin and say, "Bell, what make you so happy?"

I know many mornins he would bring his car down to me and tell me, "The mistress want you to come down early for the children." I would cook for my children and then go to her. Sometimes she used to be worried—certain problems. You know, there some things in some people— I don't know if it's the body of the person or the spirit of the person that draws some people and makes them strong. She was the weaker person—she wanted to know what made me strong. That is something that you have to really try to get it. I can remember my husband before he die, he say, "Ellen, you know something, what you have you don't keep corked, you uncork it you know." I used to be singin all day, even on the street. One day I was walkin, singin; an old man come across to me and he say, "Which church you go to?" And I say, "The Pilgrim

Holiness." It was like a seed that was sown. My grandmother always used to take me to church. My mother used to sing. So it's something perhaps I was born with.

I really love children. Only the boy kicked me once. I wasn't looking, so he give me a kick to the back of my head. But I never strike them. They love me. I used to read to them—any story that they want.

I've been here now three years. I come in on a visit. I worked, but you're not supposed to do it [without working papers]. I was in Jersey first. Then I came over here. It didn't seem strange workin in an American home because I worked for Americans in Barbados. I was never lonely because when you have God you're not alone. I carry my Bible everywhere I go. And my hymn book that we sing at church. That is what comfort me.

When I started workin in the States, the day looked different to me; the time, it looked different to me. I didn't know really the right time of the day. The changin of the climate is different than Barbados. And seasons that you go through, they're different. Bein accustomed to wakin up early,

I used to get up early and pray. The hour I get up, I meditate. I get my spiritual food before I get my natural food because the Bible say, "A man cannot live by bread alone, but by every word." I ask God to direct me, give me strength, courage, and give me faith for the day that I have to go. I get up four o'clock in the morning—I pray, and when I tire kneeling, I get up and start to sing.

When I was in Jersey, this lady I was with had a small girl. One day the mother wasn't home, and I called the girl. I said, "Look up, and you see something." I called her attention to a line from Jersey to the East—it looked like blood in the sky. She said, "Ellen, I can't look at that," and started running. I looked at it for considerable time before it vanished away. When the mother came home, she was talkin to me and I asked her if she see it. She tell me yes, she see, and it was unusual. She asked me what I think, and I say, "That is war." But you can't talk of certain things to everyone. As soon as you do, they'll say you're mad. People do not believe that God is the same God as in the Bible, and he can speak true as in the days of old.

When I got to New York, I could feel the difference of the climate through my body. And the big high buildings was really quite different. But I didn't feel nowhere strange. Why I didn't feel strange—readin the Bible I read about big cities. I can remember askin an old lady about Philadelphia—if this is the Philadelphia in the Bible. So she tell me no. But I remember Philadelphia in the Bible. People don't realize that America really is in Bible prophecy. She is in the Book of Revelations—she really is in prophecy. You read about George Washington, the Statue of Liberty—if people would read Scripture more carefully, they would see we're fulfillin our prophecy.

The Bible give me a kind of guidance. Don't mind where I am—I don't have no fear. I always read from childhood, "The wings of morning, God will be with you." See, he is with you, so why should you fear? He is really a protector. He say, "Though you walk through the valley of the shadow of death, I will fear no evil; Thy rod and staff comfort me." People think that the shadow is death, but it isn't that, it is your everyday life. You don't know when anybody goin strike you. And it happened to me, I have the experience. My husband come home at night and died beside of me. And how I managed to know—I had a dream that I see a tree full of fruits, and I went to pick one of these fruits. And just as I went to pick one of these fruits, the tree vanished, and I jump up. That was him. I jump up the same time that he was dyin, but I didn't know—I hear snorin, very deep, so I shake him and I shake him, I call him—I didn't hear no answer. So I lift that big man, I say it was the Lord that help me lift him, or the angels. It wasn't myself that put him on this pillow. He feeled so light—he feeled like when I lift this little girl here when she sometimes want me to take her up the stairs. But he had feeled so light. So you see this is an experience every woman or man have to pass through—it is somethin flowin, just like Ezekiel, Isaiah, Jeremiah.

One mornin I was over at the railroad station. I was sharin out some tracts, and a woman—I didn't know this woman was from my homeland—she looked at me. The taxi come for me, and she lookin at me, and I lookin at her. She draw me before I draw her. She called my name, she said, "Why you don't call at me, Ellen?"

I said, "Gloria?"

She said, "Ellen, you know that from the time you was small, comin up, that you was encouragin people."

So, you see, that was a witness there. I was sharin tracts to the girls at Albertson station and helpin them—their courage. Some girls tired, and they talkin about muggin, and talkin about other things, so I was givin them the tracts, and it come like a consolation and a comfort. You know, Ezekiel preached in the streets of Jerusalem, and you will see the things that Ezekiel preached—it's happening right now.

I got this job through a lady who used to work for Mrs. Rinsler's friend. So Mrs. Rinsler asked to get some person that's nice—that was me. I've been here three years now. She didn't know me; I didn't know her. She take me up at the station, and she brought me here. But the truth is, it is no change to me. I get what you call so tied up and wrapped up in the work that nothin comes strange to me. Anything that Mrs. Rinsler asks me to do—I really don't say what some girls'll say—they know they can do somethin, they say no. I don't do that. I works honest.

I wakes up early, very early, and I get my prayers. If the mother go out, I fix breakfast, but mostly, Mrs. Rinsler, she do it. Anything she want me to do, I do. Everything. If she wants sewing, I do it. I can sew. I don't tell her no lie and say, "Cannot do it." I do it. Really, housekeepin work is not easy, but it is really somethin that I like. I always love it. Andra make me very happy. She always come and love me. I love her. If her pants are too long, I shorten it. I treats them good, they treats me good. When she goes to camp, she writes me, "Ellen Rinsler." The family in Barbados, they used to call me "Ellen Bell." If anybody cannot live with me, it is that they don't want to live with me.

I understand the black girls here scream—they got angry because we come from Barbados. They tells you straight, they don't like you. I talked to one girl from California, I tell her, "We don't get angry with the people that comes from America because in our training, our government, we always have to be kind towards strangers; we have an American base there."

The American girls say we come in here and do two people work. I gets eighty-five dollars here. They say that with the washing somebody should come in and do it; the sewing, another doin it. They don't like you to do that. I can do shirts better than the laundry because we trained to do it for them. We have to do sewing, embroidery—we have to learn it, and I learn it. But these girls, they say you should not do it. But I think if you are among people, you should be a helper. So we have now become as enemies to them. I bring the Bible to them, but they don't want to hear certain parts. They trace back about the whites, what the whites used to do to them all along the South—they still talkin about that now. They say they takin their chance now, so they have this thing up against the whites. I tell them that we don't have it so in Barbados—we don't have that kind of training. If I were raised in America, I would be like them because I would perhaps know no better. What you do to my ancestors,

I should not hold you up for it. They're just talkin about what you do to my great-grandfather, great-grandmother.

Me and Mrs. Rinsler gets along all right, but we have to learn each other; human beings have to learn one another. I have a lot of friends, plenty friends, and I have plenty people too, but I always speak to God first, and I always teach my children to do that. Always carry your problems to God. He will solve them. Why you think David have sing and hum so much? You see, he encourage others by his singing—you get a melody and a joy. I have it. Although it was a hard life raisin my children, I still have what you call peace.

Laura Daniels

INTO A SAD, BEATEN SECTION OF BROOKLYN, PAST EMPTY REMNANTS OF BUILDINGS to a dreary cluster of brick projects. A wire fence to keep people off the grass. But no grass—soft-drink cans, bricks, broken glass, shredded tires, soggy cardboard cartons—pieces of things, whatever no one wanted. The elevator was grim—a tiny wired-glass peephole protected on both sides by tight iron grid work.

Laura's daughter answered the door in a soiled robe that came down over her hands. The furniture was in bad shape, but I remember a gaily painted figurine, a flamenco dancer, standing alone on the table—from time to time Laura's eyes would fall on it as we sat there. Laura appeared eager to talk, but when the interview began she froze—yes-and-no answers, or short factual responses. It was awful; I felt like an interrogator, so I turned off the tape recorder and began to tell her more about myself. At some point I told her I'd had an ulcer once, that I must have been keeping too much to myself—and she cut in, saying, "Yes, that's it!" Then she began to talk.

When she spoke about Montague, her oldest son, she dug out some color snapshots and handed them to me. There was one photo of a bunch of teen-aged boys clowning around—Montague was brandishing a knife at one of his friends, trying to maintain a fierce expression; they were all laughing. The rest of the photographs were from the funeral.

I wanted to return and speak with Laura a second time, but when I called a recording informed me that her number was no longer in service. I tried to trace her, but she'd moved on.

My name's Laura Daniels, I'm thirty-eight years old. I was raised in Warrington, North Carolina—I have two sisters there still. My father was a share farmer; he was a nice provider—he kept the place for us to live; he kept plenty food, and he was always there when we needed him as a father. He wasn't a drunkard—he never went out and stayed all night from us—not what you see now. He loved his family, loved my mother. Her and my father was very close.

My mother was the sweetest person. I guess this is why I didn't form habits like some. I never saw my mother drink; I never saw my mother curse; I never saw my mother indecent in any way; I never saw my mother with another man after my father died—my mother was just a real Christian lady. She never, she wasn't a gossipin lady. What I mean, she never talked to one lady and then tell the other lady what the other lady said. She wouldn't do that. My mother was a person that stayed home, kept a clean house, kept us clean, kept our food prepared, tried to send us to school, you know, get an education. She didn't get as much education as she'd liked—she went to seventh grade. And she tried to teach us to respect others, and told us the Bible, took us to Sunday school. She was a good homemaker, always canning. They didn't have freezers, and she would can in a jar, preserves. She was a good cook, and she made a lot of quilts—made comforters, pillowcases, sheets, crocheted by hand—she did all of this. She was really a hard worker.

My mother was thirty-eight when she married my father. He was about fifty-five. He had grandchildren from another marriage, even before he had me—I have a half-brother, he's seventy-five. In some families the father is the center, and some the mother. Don't misunderstand me, my mother was a sweet person, but it was my father I loved most. And he was the one that used to punish me—went outside and got a switch from the tree. Sometimes he would make me do it—I'd get the smallest one. I always remembered this wrong whippin I got. My brother and I got into an argument, and so he hit me and ran. I ran after him—we run round in circles. I had this pocket knife—we were peelin apples out under the tree—and when I ran, I dropped the knife. My brother came back and stepped on the knife and cut his foot. My father accused me of deliberately droppin the knife so that my brother could cut his feet. To me this was impossible, cause I could not make my brother step on this knife. I couldn't deliberately drop it, you know. Oh, I thought my father would kill me, he'd kill me cause my brother stepped on that knife. I thought that was wrong, but I couldn't tell my father so he'd believe me.

Growin up, they had the separate schools. We lived a mile up, out in the country from the main highway—and I would walk that mile to take my bus from the highway—wherein the school bus would come up the dirt road for my white friends and stop right by their house. I felt bad about that because I just didn't understand why were they any better than I was, why they got picked up and Mary and I would have to walk.

I wanted to be a nurse then—still what I wanta be, a nurse. I like takin care of the sick—black or white, it doesn't matter. In fact, I did that in the South before I left—took care of my father while he was dyin. And there wasn't welfare like it is here. After he died, I got a job to do housework, to live in with a family—to help my mother and my younger two brothers.

I did this for a few years and then met my husband when I was twenty-two. We dated for three months, and we got married. My husband had a brother in Paterson, New Jersey—Romeo. So his brother came one day. It was wintertime—there wasn't much work to do. My husband needed work, needed a job rather, so his brother asked him to come back to Paterson for a job there. He was gonna send for me. I stayed home a couple of months and waited for him to get a job and apartment. He never sent for me. Unfortunately, he turned out to be a wino. I didn't hear anything from him the whole time he was gone, but I came on North anyway—to find out where he was and what had happened. When I got to Paterson, I found that he was in the hospital—mental institution. My sister-in-law told me. So I got a sleep-in job with a doctor and his wife. While I was workin there, my husband's brother got him out of the hospital and sorta like signed him over, and I was responsible for him. So when he came out, he would call where I was workin, and he would come to the lady's house. This made me nervous because he would always come drinkin. The lady would be nervous because she didn't know what to expect—and this made me nervous for her. With me and my husband the lady would try to, you know, leave me free for my husband. Like if he came out on the job, and he wanted me to be with him, she would give me privilege to leave or talk to him. And he wasn't earnin any money, so I had to give him some from my pay—and he spent it on drink. Then he wanted me to live with him, so that was the reason I gave up this job. I felt funny—I felt nervous, shaky, painful—I was just miserable.

This lady had been good to me, but I couldn't tell her how I was feelin. I don't know what you would call it—I guess it's an inferior—I have a feelin, I just don't express my feelin to people, you know. Even though I'm with em. I keep my feelin within myself, which is bad. It was always the question who—who would understand me? Who would wanta hear my problems, you know? Who would believe me? You know, because I feel like it's—I even got sick from it—high blood pressure and tension because I keep so much within myself. But I would, you know, let out a little at a time. I still don't express my whole feelins. I don't know, I just can't do it because I feel conscious of other peoples. I feel like, why should

I tell? I feel like the next person have problems like I have, and I feel like they don't want to hear me, they don't want to listen to me. Even now, I got problems within myself I would never discuss with the minister.

I never felt like I was important like other people, and what always happened, I always got betrayed. I had high hopes—get married, he'd get a little job, I'd get an education, buy us a home. Live happy—you know, come out properly. Bein poor I wanted to live a little better. My husband was a high school graduate, and he had two years of college. So I had looked for quite a future, you know. And this is what happens all the time, seem like. Every time, look for a future and—terrible. I always wanted an education; I looked forward to that. And to me this is another thing keep me in this shell—because I never had an education. Bein around educated peoples, it sorta puts you, you know, in a shell. You always thought about what they were gonna think about you—a dummy, you know, you're uneducated, or you're poor. You know, I feel why tell you all of these things, because I felt like nothin that happened to me was interestin to anybody. Although good things have happened to me, I didn't feel like they were interestin to anyone else. Because, like I say—goin round, doubletalkin—my childhood was real nice. Bein a child—horses, I used to like to ride horseback on the farm. But then I wanted city life. I wanted to get away from the farm because I'd been raised there. Like my children now, they want a country life. When they grow up, they don't want any parts of the city. They're goin back to the country, they think. But I wanted the city life for myself.

I really wasn't hopin for a good marriage. It was a good education that I always wanted. Marriage wasn't my ideal—it was my mother's. They wanted me to get married. My mother didn't trust me into comin to the city without a husband. She figured I would come here—she heard so many bad things about the city—I would, you know, turn out to be the worst person in the world. She always said I was wild. She wouldn't approve of me to come here alone, so I had to get married to come to the city. In the country, once you married you expect a future, somethin different. You get married, you get a job, you have a husband to help you, you get a home, then a car—you begin to live better. That's what the country peoples expected of you. And then after that, it was an embarrassment. I stayed on with my husband five years. I left him off and on, and went back. He would promise me he would get better, stop drinkin, be a husband. And he didn't. So I left him altogether. He's still drinkin—he's in Boston with his mother.

My work was always enjoyable. I always enjoyed livin in with these families. It was like one big family, you know, because the majority of the families I worked with, they was like you or me. Color didn't make any difference. I mean, they treated me as one of the family. This is why I always enjoyed domestic work. I always could get along, and I was fortunate to find people who liked black people. Then, I would have my room. The whole house would feel like it was mine. I would enjoy their home as if it was mine. I worked as if it was mine, and I was always free to go to the refrigerator to take anything I wanted to eat. They just gave me free privilege, and I enjoyed it. My children were babies back then, and I would have a babysitter or neighbor help me. I accepted it, as I had to work. I always worked in my life, and now, we have welfare, it's a hard thing to sit and not to work—but my pastor thinks I need to be home with my children until they grow up a little more. But I find it hard to accept money and not earn it. I guess because I was brought up this way. I like to earn mine—I done it all my life. And I like homemakin; it's somethin I enjoy. I enjoy the beauty of homes. To me it's an art—it really was interestin, the beauty of it.

In New Jersey I would speak on the telephone or write my family, but I never was lonely. I always could make friends. That never was a problem with me. White, black—maybe this sounds strange, but a white person was more my friend because somehow the black would always, you know, look on you as if I was poor, uneducated. I guess you wonder why this happened. My older brothers, they all expected more from me than what actually happened. Their children went to college. Because I didn't do it, they kinda look down on me—I guess this what started it. And your family can hurt worse than anyone else, you know. Because strangers —you sorta get over that because they were a stranger—but here your sisters and your brothers do it to you—it's hard to get over it. I only have one brother that I'm very close to—he lives in Norfolk, Virginia. He understands. And this is my reason for not expressin myself—because I don't feel like everyone understands, or want to understand, or try to understand. But the white people—the more educated they were, and the more they hold, the more humble they would feel to me. Like I can feel more relaxed now, though you told me you was a educated man. I feel— although it's strange what I'm doin—I feel relaxed. I don't feel that you— because I can't place my words—that you are lookin down on me, or are thinkin that I'm a dummy. That's the way they have treated me.

When I lived in New Jersey, I came visitin twice to New York. Then I met this man. He was a friend of this lady who rented me an apartment, and they used to come and drink together, and I was there. I got to know him, and then I moved out and got my own apartment, and he would come by my place. I was in love with him—well, I didn't get any love from him either. He was even worse than my husband. I met him, and he became—he was a violent man. He became jealous, vicious, threatenin— filled with threats, because he thought—he was livin with another woman, and she found out he was datin me, so she left him and went back to Alabama. So when she left, he accused me of drivin her away—broke up his happy home and family—and I had to live with threats. I couldn't take it because he threatened me with this gun—he said he was gonna kill me, and I thought he would. It scared me. I didn't want to have this gun at my heart. He was gonna blow my heart out—and I was always afraid of a gun. So I decided to leave him, and I came to Brooklyn runnin from him. He didn't know a thing about Brooklyn—couldn't find me. This been ten years ago.

Brooklyn, Brooklyn is—it looks like home, it really feels home. I feel that home feelin. When I first came, it was the dirtiest place I ever saw, but I like it. I still like it. I've worked on and off for a lotta families that was good to me. One that didn't work out so well was these Irish people— mother and two daughters. Mother was about ninety-five—and they rich. They're just lovely when I first started, but then they began to feel that I was a machine—just somebody in the house, just work, work, work. As if I was a child. They had no feelin for me. Although I was doin all I could do for this mother and the daughters. One daughter was in a wheelchair. They was very unfortunate—all her children was affected by polio. One was affected in the mind—that's the one give me such a hard time workin for them. But then all of the love that I would try to show for her mother—somehow or other this daughter would just, you know, turn her nose up and mistreat me. They had no consideration of me havin a family. If I would ask a day to be off to do somethin, they would call up and say, "Come in this time, I want you here." I couldn't be with my family; I had no time for my children.

They made me feel like nobody—black. You know, my color—even the dogs would be treated better than me. And I could see this, they were showin this to me. When it came to feedin me, they would give the dogs better—not that I cared so much, but it was showin me how much you appreciate all the love I was givin for her mother. Their mother really loved me—she's sick, a senile person—and I love carin for people. But the dogs were gettin more love. They'd go out and buy the dogs somethin nice every day. But me, I got leftovers. They'd make the dog a hamburger, or chicken leg, or somethin like that—wherein, "Laura, this bread is stale; old Marge won't want that, so you can have this." In other words, after keepin somethin three or four days, I can eat it. The animals were a mess. They had eight cats and two dogs, and they talked to them a lot. They were their children—they treated them as though they were children. But me—they had nothing to say to me—but the cats, you know, they kissed the cats. Me?—"Laura, don't sing now, don't——" You speak with a pleasant face—they walk around with a sour face all the time. You didn't know what to say and what not to say. You say somethin, she might snap your head off. I just walked around the house in a shell. I got so nervous—I was sick the whole year.

They treated me bad, yes, they treated me bad. And I didn't want to talk about it—I wanted to keep it within myself, you know. How you gonna tell nobody? I was so glad to have a job, doin what I like to do—and that's workin with the elderly people, makin people comfortable. I think I started out like this—I got the idea of bein a nurse cause my father had cancer. He died of cancer. He was in an institution, and they sent him home to be with us to die. My mother wanted him to die at home, and he lived two weeks at home with us. My father was close to me, and my father was always good to me, never mistreated me. I think that's why when a man hurt me, it did somethin to me—cause my father had never did it to me. And I used to sit by my father to try to make him comfortable—rub his back, keep him turned over, just keep him comfortable. And I enjoyed that. This is why I wanted to become a nurse. This is just in me—I don't feel like I've accomplished nothin unless I could help somebody. I feel if I had a typin job in a office, I wouldn't be helpin. I'd like a job where I could help someone.

I kept findin steady work till two years ago when the police shot my oldest son. Montague was seventeen at the time, and nobody never told me really what happened. I think it was his friends that—you know, sometime you get with the wrong people. And I think it was that. He had warnings. He had been in trouble, but not to reform school. He would always be with the crowd that do something, and I would have to go to court with him. He would always be innocent—the judge would find him not guilty. He had a girlfriend, and he would stay out two or three nights a week. It upset me—it's very terrible, because I expected this was gonna happen with all the violence and crime and young people and shootin. But when it happened, I wasn't surprised. The times that I were upset, it didn't happen; when it happened, I was all calm and relaxed. He came home this Friday, so I asked him to go with me someplace, and he said he had a party to go to. He got ready, dressed, and went out. It was two o'clock. So six o'clock this night, twenty-third of May, his girlfriend called cryin. I thought they had had a fight. So she told me Montague had got shot. I asked her who shot him, so she said the housing police that was standin on the street.

They had a write-up about it—I think I lost it—in the *Amsterdam News*. The cop said he had a knife, but it was never even more mention about a knife or gun. And she told me that Montague had got shot—they had called an ambulance and taken him to the hospital, Kings County. So I went out to Kings County, and I asked to see a young man that had got shot by the policeman—and they said he was in the mortuary. So my girlfriend—me and Sonia went to the mortuary—so he's there dead. And he was buried the thirtieth of May.

You don't get any understandin. The police never came by to say why or what happened. I understand that he was the wrong person—police was after someone else. These are the stories that I heard. I never found out definitely who they were really after, cause the police never came. I never looked for a lawyer—too much trouble. I thought—here we're livin in city houses, and, you know, what could I do with the city? I didn't think it was worth tryin—although it was my son. I loved him so dearly. I love em all, but to me he was really special.

I worried for him, cause Brownsville was a dangerous place for young people—a lot of gangs, you know, was formed there. And I think he was a part—he told me he wasn't with em, but I felt like he was still with the gangs. He was charged with theft one time—boys stole this man's car—and I went to court for him. But he said he didn't know what was goin on. Then there was a case of rape. His friend raped some guy, and Montague was standin by waitin for the friend to come out. The one that did the rapin told the police that Montague was with em, so they came for him again. It's a long story, but through all of this—even with all of this—he never left Brownsville. And I figured sooner or later somethin bad was gonna happen. I talked to him and talked to him and talked to him—he wouldn't listen, he had a girlfriend. Hardest thing in my life have been men.

Before the police shot Montague, I got saved and turned to the Lord so that I wouldn't have to have problems again. Now I enjoy goin to church, readin the Sunday book. This is my life now. This is why I was able to go through it with Montague—because if I hadn't had His strength, I woulda been in the crazyhouse by now. My mind woulda snapped, I know it. I couldn't of stood it. I repented of my sins; then I got baptized in Jesus' name, and I continued to go to church and learn about the Lord, which I'm doin now—more about what the Lord required me to do. It's the Whole Truth Church of Jesus Christ. We have service four times a week. All of my children go.

Sometime the boys are very lonely here with me—and I would like a nice man for their sake. But that touch-and-go thing is still there, you know. Maybe he would be good to me for a year or so—cause this what happens—maybe he's so nice for a year—and all of a sudden there's a change, there's a turn—they become violent. You know, to me men always take advantage of me because I was never a violent woman. I never fight or curse or use them. And when a man hits me, I'm very fearful and I don't fight back. Other women say they would fight back—I never was a violent woman. I never saw this in my home, and it grew up in me. I always liked love, affection. I have lived for it. This way has kept me runnin all the time because once I love a person, or a person's goin to love me and get by with me, then I would leave him rather than to fight. So after gettin my youngest child, I'd rather not to get involved with men—cause where else could I leave to? I didn't wanta go nowhere. I was tired of travelin, I wanted to settle down. I want a man to give a helpin hand, but who? This is always the question—who? I'm really afraid to trust anyone. So I enjoy goin to church, and I make the best of it, you know. Get my strength in it, so to speak.

Now I work two days and spend the other time at home because I noticed my work has an effect on my children's schoolin. Jimmy has failed in his education quite a bit, and I think it's because the fear of comin home and not findin Momma in the house. Before, when I worked, I leave home at eight-thirty and it's six o'clock before I could get home. And I did this five days a week. I want to see the children grow up, get an education, get a job. And me, for me, I want to still fulfill my desire—go to school and get a nurse's aid—to be able to work in a hospital or nursing home.

I've had my bad life. Rough. But I'm glad I'm able to smile and look for a future. I'm glad I don't have to face people with all whatever happened to me on my face—you know, take it out on other people. Some people does that, I think, and that's what I'm always skeptical of doin—burden people. I just, I don't like to burden people in no way. That's something I never want to be to anybody, not even my children. It's a pleasure for me to do anything in my power that I can do for a person—comb their hair, file, clean their nails out, feed them, wash their face—you know, sick person can't wash their face. It's my pleasure to see them lookin better, feelin better. And happy—if I can make a person happy, I like to do that. Then I'm happy. So when my time come for help, I hope somebody give me that same attitude I give in my work—you understand me? When they're doin it for me, whatever they have to do for me, I hope they won't give me an impression that it's a burden. I want to feel they be doin it with joy and pleasure. See, that's what I do for anybody—I does it with joy and pleasure.

Irene Larsen

I found the number of Larsen's Employment Agency in the yellow pages, and when I explained my project to Mrs. Larsen she was full of enthusiasm and agreed to help. Over the next three weeks I spent a number of hot summer mornings in the reception area of her agency hoping to make contact with household workers. My visits led to only a few interviews, but my days at the agency were useful as a kind of initiation into my work. Sitting there, in the midst of women waiting to be interviewed, I felt the peculiar tension of anticipation. Some of the women talked to one another and others thumbed through magazines, but most looked toward Mrs. Larsen's desk, expectant, anxious to find work. Mrs. Larsen dispatched each woman in a few minutes, but she communicated an interest and respect that seemed to assure each woman she would find her suitable placement. When she spoke with prospective employers over the phone, there was no change in her voice or manner. Before anyone left the office to visit an employer's home for an interview, Mrs. Larsen always made certain they had money for transportation and clear directions on how to find the address. And she made it clear that the women could call her anytime they needed a sympathetic counselor.

When I sat down to speak with Mrs. Larsen, she received a call from an employer who was terribly upset to learn that her maid was married. "Shouldn't she be home with her husband?" the employer asked. "She'd love being home with her husband and children," Mrs. Larsen assured her, "but they're poor; they need money; they can't get by on welfare." The employer demanded to know why the husband wasn't working, and Mrs. Larsen explained that the man had been laid off, that these were hard times for the poor, that jobs are not easy to come by. The conversation went on like this for a few minutes and ended with Mrs. Larsen patiently repeating that the household worker wanted to help her family survive, that she had no training for blue-collar work, that this was the work she knew best. When the conversation ended, she turned to me and said, "Now that lady is a perfectly nice individual, but you see how little she understands. Sometimes I have to spell everything out for them; they have no idea what it is to be poor. I get this all the time."

I'm Irene Larsen. I'm presently the manager for Larsen's Employment Agency in White Plains. I was born in Memphis, Tennessee in 1915.

My father had a very good job with the Frisco Railroad for forty-eight years, and my mother was always a housewife—she never worked. Our situation was very unusual for the South—my mother was white and my father was black. They never told me much about how they met, because parents didn't talk about those things then. My mother's mother raised four children alone, so I suppose the financial situation prompted my mother to marry. I never knew my mother's family—except for one sister who also married a black man. We lived in a black area, and my light color was just overlooked. Most of my friends were in our neighborhood—I had many playmates who had the same color skin as I did. They were in the same situation as a result of interracial marriages—not necessarily marriages, but illegitimate, you know.

School was a nightmare for me. I couldn't exist in the public-school system, because in those days it was all black—and being as light as I am, I was discriminated against by black people. The children in school would throw rocks at me and push me. They knew I was black—I never pretended to be anything else—but they resented the color of my skin. My parents would tell me that the people didn't know any better and that I shouldn't feel badly, but many days I would come home from school crying. I remember one time I brought a black friend with me to Catholic church. We sat down in the church, and we were asked to move and stand in the back of the church. It was a very bad experience for me—I went home crying. When I went with my mother, we always took a seat, but with my black friend along—to think that with all the empty seats, I had to stand in the back! I didn't go back to that church anymore.

I couldn't live with the discrimination that was leveled against me in those days. That's why I went to private school. It was mostly white professional families who sent their children—and no one treated me badly. They were more tolerant, and there were *more of me*, my images, in the school. I was lucky I was able to go to a private school—there were many of my friends who didn't, who suffered. A lot of friends who grew up with that pressure won't admit they are black now. I didn't feel any superiority to darker-colored blacks, but many of my friends did, unfortunately. Many friends passed and are married to whites now—just kept it secret—people who hold very high positions in Washington and other places. And there are many, many people of my color, black people, that I can point out on the subway every morning—people on the borderline. We know each other—there's something about it. We have, I don't know, sort of a connection going.

After I got married we moved to New York. In New York I stayed home for many years, because I have six children and I wanted to be there to raise them—but I worked on and off in my husband's agency for twenty-six years. At first I did contact work—I went to big firms to get job listings for the agency. And then I was really passing—I'll be perfectly honest. I wanted them to think that I was white, because I was after jobs. But that's the only time I've ever wanted to pass. I never lied. I just presented myself as I was and let them use their own imagination.

What I do here now is sell jobs—I get employees for employers. In this type of work you have to definitely be a salesman. This is what it's all about. It's sales. You're selling the employee to the employer; you're selling the employer to the employee—and I think both are *equally* important. It's just as important to let the employee know what they're getting into as it is to let the employer know what he's getting. The employer has the money, it's true, but without the employee he can't make it. This is true not only for domestic work but for commercial and industrials. We have them all, all types of jobs.

I am honest. That's the secret in this business—being honest. In many instances I could rig up fictitious references, but it would be to my detriment. Suppose I rig up a reference on an employee who goes out to someone's home and steals. Then I'm in trouble. I've had instances—not too many—where there has been theft of jewelry, silver, and clothing—but I wasn't called on it because I had checked references, and there was none of this in the person's past work experience. We do not accept written references. I get many people who hand me letters over the desk that I know full well a friend of theirs wrote. Anybody can write a letter. And I found, too, that employers aren't always honest in giving references. I've had people give me very good references for people who don't know how to run a vacuum cleaner. We telephone former employers and fill out a standard form. We ask, is the person honest? That's the most important. Is she competent? Is she reliable? Are they competent in cooking? In cleaning? In child care? Most employers will say, "Yes, yes, yes." Or, "Oh, she's very nice!" But then we go and say, "Would you recommend her for employment to a friend of yours?" And that's what gets them. Sometimes they'll just say, "Well, no, I don't think she's quite capable." We get true answers then.

We interview all our employees here in the office. We're not supposed to ask age, but we like to have some indication as to approximately how old you are—where are you from?—what is your education?—are you married?—do you have children?—are you rooming, or do you have your own apartment?—how did you hear of this agency?—your credit references—what you did on your previous jobs—did you clean?—did you do any cooking?—was it child care?—how old were the children?—did you feed the children?—did you bathe them?—did you have to put them to bed?—did you baby-sit?—did you like your job? We gain a lot of insight into that person's personality just by asking these questions. I can tell very well—if I ask, "How old were the children?" and she says, "Oh, I don't remember how old they were"—she doesn't like children. If you like children, you're going to remember how old those children were. I have some people say, "Oh, Vivien was such a lovely child! She was three years old when I went there, but when I left she was four and one half." This indicates to me that this person likes children. If I worked for six months, I would know the age of the child, and I would assume they would, if they cared anything about children. So this is how we get a picture of the person.

When we find an employer we feel that person is good for, we call the employer, tell the employer the basic background of the employee, and arrange for them to meet them. Sometimes they come to the office, but in most instances they go to the home, because we feel the employee would like to see where they're going to live, meet the children, see the reaction of the children, and see if the house is too big. There are many aspects that the employee has to be pleased about as well as the employer. Many agencies do not set up home interviews. I call to get train schedules and bus schedules, and to find how much the fare is, because frequently the fares run to four dollars. Some of these people may not have the money, so why should they go to Penn Station and get turned back at the ticket window? They've lost fifty cents in bus fare now, and fifty cents to many of these people is very important. So I try to get as much information to them as possible—and our agency asks that the employer pay the fare for interviews.

You know, I have many people tell me that I'm very adaptable to any type of situation in this business. Here's where my childhood experience helped me. I definitely gained from all that—it learned me to live in the world. Here I'm in the middle between employee and employer. Many times I have to make decisions as to who's right and who's wrong when I hear a situation discussed. For instance, I had a report of theft from an employer—it happened to have been a dress that was packed in a box of food that was being discarded. I agreed that the employee did the wrong thing to take anything without permission, but on the other hand I sort of sympathized with the employee, because she probably wanted the dress very badly and she probably thought—"Well, she no longer wants it; she's getting ready to give it away, so why shouldn't I have it?" I cannot place the employee again because she did take something without permission. But it wasn't a real theft—I don't feel that it was. It has put me in a sort of precarious position—the girl is a good girl, and she's a good worker, and I hate to lose her, but if I place her and she decides to do this again then *I'm* in trouble.

I have employers call and tell me, "Please send me someone that can be part of my family." And I think that people realize that to have a successful relationship they have to treat people decent. I had a woman come to me—she's stayed on her job for one week. She apologized profusely for leaving the job, but she said, "Mrs. Larsen, I was in the basement—the dog slept in my room, he did his business in my room, and I just couldn't stand the smell."

I said, "Well, you don't need to apologize."

That employer was making this woman feel that she's no better than the dog. It's a psychological fact. I put this on the employer's card—and the next person I have for this lady, I will tell her that in order to keep an employee she will have to find another place for the dog, because I can't send anyone else. I don't care who they are, no one is going to want to sleep with a dog.

Like I said before—I'm very honest, and I have to be. I have employees who come to me with body odor, and I will tell them, "I can't send you out until you use a deodorant." You just have to be honest. Many times people are not aware—they just don't know any better, especially when they first come here. It all boils down to being honest. I've had employees walk off the job because something took place that they didn't like. And

I told these people, "If there's something you don't like, sit down and talk about it. Don't be afraid, don't get angry—tell your employer you don't like to do such-and-such a thing, that you don't like to pick up dirty underwear, you don't like to stay up until eleven o'clock at night doing dinner dishes. Tell them, 'Have a little sympathy for me, because I must get up at seven o'clock to fix your breakfast, and you don't have to.' "

It's hard for many employers to perceive the difficulties that employees are encountering in this inflated world—how hard it is for these women to find enough money to exist. And, for instance, it's hard for a southern woman from, say, North Carolina, to accept the treatment she gets from northern employers. Southern employers make you feel at home. You may not eat at the table with them, but in most instances you eat at the same time. Most New York families require service—you take the food to and from the kitchen and serve them. But in the South they eat family-style, with the food on the table. In many jobs the employer does the cooking, and I've had women quit jobs because they didn't like the food. "I'm starved, Mrs. Larsen," they tell me.

We get a lot of homesickness. Women leave their children in their countries to come here to work because there's no work where they live. They make the sacrifice to come here, so they can send money to their families in the Islands. This is a big problem. I have employers calling me—"She cried all night, Mrs. Larsen. I can't stand it! She should go home to her family." And I have a lot of sympathetic employers who will urge the person to go back home. I had a person work for me once that cried and cried. I would take her out shopping; I did everything to pacify her, but she wasn't satisfied until I brought her son here—one of her children, just one.

Maybe the biggest problem our women face is the working hours. Some women tell me they get up at seven in the morning and don't go to bed until ten or eleven at night. I think there should be a law stating that you're not working straight through the day. If she gets up at seven in the morning, then she should have her rest period between twelve and three and then do the laundry et cetera until dinner time. Then after dinner she should be able to go to bed by eight. But the idea that you've got to stay up till ten or eleven is turning everybody off. I have women come here and tell me, "Before I sleep in again, I'll go hungry! They work you too hard, Mrs. Larsen; I cannot work from seven A.M. until eleven P.M.—and this is what some people expect." Many people need a sleep-in domestic, to have someone in the house baby-sitting in case they have to go out—not necessarily sitting up, but being near enough to where the children are sleeping so that if anything happens they can hear the child. But the idea—I've had some women tell me that they've had to sit up until two or three o'clock in the morning to wait for their employer to come home, because the employer didn't want them to go to sleep while the children were out. I say, "Well, do they stay up with the children when they are home? They don't stay up all night listening for the children, so why don't you tell them that."

The majority of our placements now are from the Islands, the West Indies, Central and South America. Very few of our domestics were born in the North, and many southern Americans are not doing domestic work any longer. There are many illegal aliens doing domestic work. It's the only means of meeting the demand for domestic help. The only way I will place a person who is not here legally is when I find an employer who promises to sign an application to grant them their legal residence. I'm doing the papers for many of them right now myself. And now the Labor Department is granting certification for more domestics, because they too realize that there are few domestics available.

There are some employers who waste my time and money. I have at least three thousand dollars that I'm unable to collect from employers who hire a girl, use her three or four weeks, and refuse to pay the agency.

We keep a record. I've had people call me back years later, and I go to the file and say, "You hired this girl, and you kept her four weeks, and you never paid me any money. That has to be paid before I can send you someone else." After all, this is a very reputable agency—I'm an egoist to that extent—but we have to work at it. There's this one woman who's been calling—an elderly woman who needs care, a semi-invalid. I have sent her twelve people, but I think she's mental—with my experience I should have known after only three. But she calls me so pathetically—"Please Mrs. Larsen, send me help—I need someone so bad"—you know. I sent a person yesterday and she says, "The woman spoke beautiful English." Today she tells me the woman doesn't speak English. I just put her card up there to be filed away. She can call me as many times as she wishes—I'm not wasting my time or the person's time anymore.

The going wage for what we call day work is three dollars an hour plus the carfare. I instituted this myself about six months ago. Previous to that it was two-fifty an hour. I get many people calling me now wanting to pay two dollars an hour, and I will not accept that job order. On a weekly basis the wages run between ninety dollars and one hundred and fifty dollars. When people say, "What are domestics getting today?" I will say, "It depends on the duties. How many are in the family? How big a house do you have? How much work is involved?" If it's a large house and a large family, and they have to do the cooking, one hundred and fifty dollars should be the wage. Not many people are paying it though—I'll be perfectly honest. As for work benefits—if I told employers they had to offer two weeks' paid vacation, Blue Cross–Blue Shield, and life insurance, I'd go out of business. Many employers are very fair. I've had many tell me that they give a week's vacation after a year, two weeks after two years, and that they give paid holidays. One or two have said that after six months they pay Blue Cross–Blue Shield. So I think the idea is sort of getting across to some employers. These demands for work benefits should be publicized because you have a lot of really sensitive employers in the domestic world that are very anxious to do what is right by their fellow man—they are humanitarians. Others will never get the idea—many people will do without help rather than pay benefits that the women need. A lot of these people can't afford domestic help to begin with—that's why you get people paying seventy-five dollars and eighty-five dollars a week. They can't afford to pay any more, so they're taking advantage, they're exploiting.

Rose Marie Hairston

Rose Marie Hairston's apartment was on 102nd Street just west of Central Park. The shells of three abandoned cars gave the kids on the block a prop for their various games. None of the locks worked on the front door of her building; all the mailboxes had been jimmied open. The smell of urine, garbage, decay. Before our interview began, Rose explained to me that there had been three fires in her building in the past month. The way she saw it, her landlord preferred to collect on fire insurance rather than throw away money on legally required maintenance and repairs. She would have to find a new place soon because the city was about to condemn the building. She laughed as she told all this to me, and her laughter puzzled me. Her fight with the landlord was frustrating, infuriating, and exhausting. There seemed nothing funny about that.

Later, as Rose began to recount her personal history, Donna Jaykita, her eleven-year-old daughter, came to the kitchen door and listened. She enjoyed her mother's stories, and Rose Marie seemed more comfortable delivering her narrative to a familiar face. For the most part Donna Jaykita was perfectly silent, but a few times she broke into laughter, usually in response to a story in which her mother had suffered some indignity. Through her laughter Donna Jaykita acknowledged that her mother's message had been received and understood. There was a daughter's love in these moments, as well as recognition of the pressures she would have to face as a black woman in America. This led me back to Rose's laughter, which had seemed so out of place before. Now it seemed her laughter rose up against the whole dreary mess; it came from a tough, defiant sense of herself, a sign that some part of her stubbornly remained free from her circumstances, and that as a result, no crisis would get the best of her.

I'm Rose Marie Hairston. I am thirty-eight years old. I was born in Virginia—Martinsville, Virginia. There's mostly furniture factories, farmin, tobacco there. My family had their own house, but we didn't live there all the time. Well, my parents moved to West Virginia, and my father was a motorman in the coal mine and a brakeman. A motorman works the little car that you drive down in the mine to bring the coal out. Sometimes he was a brakeman, and he would ride on the back of the little car, which was very dangerous. From workin in the mine and the water he got fluid in his knees and fluid in his elbows and up in his shoulder. And from gettin his back hurt and his hip hurt six or seven times, it caused him to have a type of arthritis. My father started workin at the coal mine at the age of fourteen, and he was retired about the time he got forty. He had been hurt a lotta times, you know; he was all broken up.

I was a good-sized girl when he retired. We couldn't afford to buy coal, so we used to have to go in some of the strip mines an get the coal. Well, you know some people could afford it, but we were very poor, very poor, a very poor family after my father retired. Sometimes we couldn't get in the mines cause they had a watchman, so we would have to go over on the Chesapeake and Ohio Railroad and wait for the train car to come by. The cars used to be loaded with coal, so my brother and I would jump the train and get on the car and throw off enough coal. They had a railroad detective, so sometimes they would catch us. They would ask us about the coal, and we would tell them no, we was just playin, just jumpin on the train an ridin the train. They would tell us it was very dangerous, you know; you could get your leg cut off, or you would be thrown under the car. But it was fun for us. On Sunday we used to go in the mine and play cowboy and Indians, different little games. It was dark and you couldn't see, you had to feel your way around. Sometimes we used to like to go in and kill bats.

In West Virginia we never knew anything about predjudice or the racial whatever-you-call-it. Really, we didn't never heared anything about that until we grew up an went back to the state of Virginia. Where we lived, around the coal mine, there was Jews, Italians, Hungarians, Polacks, an just about any race you could name. Everybody mingled together. Really, we never heard of all this mess until we grew up. When I was about ten my brother Maurice and me went back to Virginia on the farm for a summer. We didn't know what they were talkin about when they used to say "colored people." In West Virginia we didn't use the word "colored people." Everybody there was together. But when we were goin to Virginia, we got off the bus to go to the bathroom, and we wanted somethin to eat, and we saw a sign said "Colored in the Rear." We went in there—it was a little, dirty, greasy room about the size of a good chicken house. It was so dirty in there. And then we wondered why all the white people were sittin up in the best part of the bus. Even the bathrooms said "No Colored." Even the telephones had big signs that said "No Colored."

My grandfather, who lived in Virginia, was workin for Judge Whittle, so we stayed there and worked for him awhile. Still, you could tell there was a lot of prejudice there too. I always wondered why he always called my grandfather "Uncle William" and he called my grandmother "Aunt Dycie." I used to ask my brother, "What he call Grandpa 'Uncle William' for? That's not his uncle." Maurice said, "I don't know why they do that." We ran into trouble one day. We went to the judge's brother's house to do some work. His brother had this little eight-year-old girl and her name was Ruth. So we went around to speak to Ruth and we said, "Hi, Ruth, pleased to meet ya!" And my oldest brother, Raymond, who lived there with my grandfather all the time, said, "You have to call her Miss Ruth."

I said, "We got to call her *Miss* Ruth?"

He said, "Yeah."

I said, "Well, I ain't gonna call her Miss Ruth!"

And my brother Maurice said, "Well, I ain't gonna call her no Miss Ruth, that's a little girl! Momma told us don't call nobody no mister or missus down here!"

Raymond said, "You have to call her Miss Ruth, cause if you don't call her Miss Ruth, they'll take you off and beat you!"

I said, "Well, I don't think anybody can beat us!" cause we thought we could beat anybody.

We just didn't like callin the little children miss and mister. Judge Whittle had a little boy named Kenneth, but we had to call him Mr. Kenneth and say "Yes sir" and "No sir." We hadn't been used to that; so finally my brother got a kerosene lamp one night, and we slipped into the doghouse where my grandmother and grandfather couldn't see us, and we wrote a letter to my mother. We told her that we had to say "Yes sir" and "No sir" to children, and when they wanted you to do something they called you "boy" or "girl" or "nigger." And we didn't like it.

One time they had a big cattle show. Raymond, Maurice, and myself thought we was gonna walk around like the other people, but all the black people there was the people that was workin. They wasn't goin around buyin anything, an we couldn't understand it cause we had some nickels to buy things with. So this great big fat red-faced white man came out and said, "Hey, come here!" And I looked at my brother and said, "Who's he talkin' to?"

Maurice said, "He's talkin to us. Let's go over and see what he wants. Maybe he wants us to do some work, and we can git some money."

So we went over to see what he wanted, and he gave us a shovel. My brother said, "What you want me to do with this?"

The man said, "I just want you to take the shovel, and go behind the cows, and every time they drop a pile, you pick up the pile in the shovel."

So my brother said, "My momma told us before we left to go here, 'Don't you all go bein a flunky for nobody!' My momma told me not to come over here, runnin behind no cows and things like that."

So the man said he would see that we did it, and he went and got my grandfather. My grandfather told us to take the shovel cause there was a job to do, so we stayed and did it for about half a second. And this man come out and gave us a box of cherry candy, which didn't excite me or my brother Maurice, but it excited the hell out of Raymond. Then we sneaked off and came back home. We told my mother—and she said that Raymond had to do it cause he lived there, and we didn't have to do it cause we didn't live there and didn't understand it.

When I was a little girl, I always had hopes of bein a nurse or a doctor. One of my sisters, she wanted to be a doctor, too. She had hopes of bein a doctor. Another one wanted to be a nurse, and one wanted to be a schoolteacher. We'd say that one day we'd be the Hairston Clinic. We always wanted somethin that would help others. One time we said we'd work and make a lotta money, and then we'd go back to West Virginia and have an orphanage. Unfortunately, it never happened.

I was about sixteen and a half, and I was readin a newspaper. It said, "Ladies and Girls 18 and over: Jobs in New York." And you didn't even have to pay to come to New York. This ad said it paid one hundred and twenty-five dollars a week. I said, "Oh boy, that's good! I think I'll go up there and talk to this man." He was a preacher too, and that's what made me mad. It was jus another ol gimmick. Anyway, I went up there an he interviewed me. He said, "How old are ya?" I told him I was eighteen, and he kept lookin at me. He said, "I don't know, Rose, you look very young. Matter of fact, you look like you're no more than twelve." I said, "No, eighteen." So he told me to bring him proof that I was eighteen, or bring my mother. I told him all right. I caught the bus and went back home and got my cousin to come back with me. She was a much older lady than I was. She told them that she was my mother. She gave her consent for me to come to New York. So he said all right. He told me to come the next day and that he would meet me at the bus station. Then he described the persons that were to meet me in New York on Fiftieth Street. So I met him the next day, and he gave me the bus ticket and he said, "Good luck, Rose." I said, "Yeah." And he said, "When you make all that money, put it in the bank." I wasn't scared; I was determined because I thought one hundred and twenty-five dollars a week was a long ways from bein seven-fifty a week.

I didn't tell my mother I was goin. She kept askin, "Where you goin?"

I said, "I'm goin over to visit somebody for a little while."

She said, "I think the right thing for you to do is ask me to give you permission to go. You don't just get ready and go."

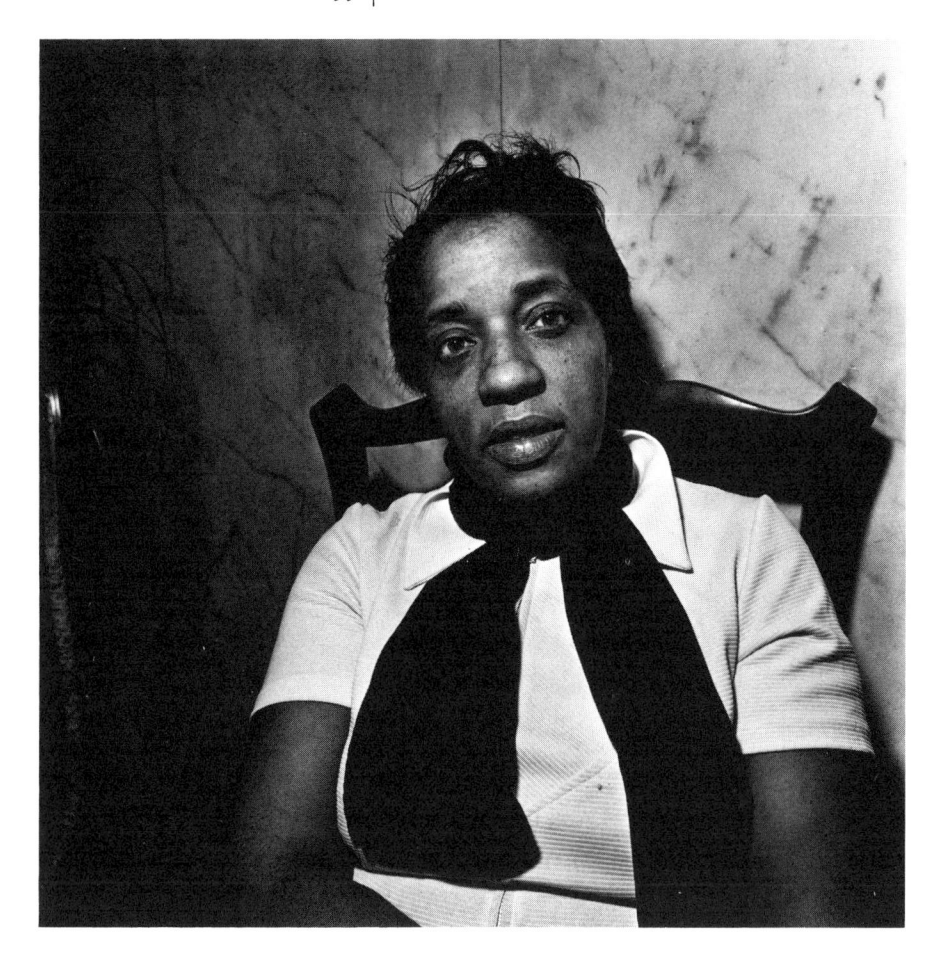

I said, "I want to go visit a friend over in Lewisburg."

"Well, all right. But you don't need a suitcase just to take two or three dresses, do you?"

I said, "No."

She said, "Well, you can put em in this ol brown shopping bag." She give me this little brown shopping bag to put the three dresses in and some underpants and bras. She asked me, "You want me to go to the station with you?"

I said, "No, I'm a big girl, I can catch a bus."

She said, "When you get there, you call back." There wasn't but one telephone in the neighborhood, so everybody knew your business. She told me to call back Miss Wilson and tell Miss Wilson that I had got there all right.

I went over to the bus station and met the preacher, Brother Plow. He was there with my bus ticket. I jumped on the bus. I was so excited. I was lookin out the windows, an I was listenin good for the man to say New York. I was so excited. I said to myself, "Ooooh, now I get to see the movie stars!" I thought you'd probably see them on the streets. I had read a book about Harlem, and I was dyin to see Harlem—Hundred-Twenty-fifth Street, the Apollo Theater, and I was dyin to see Forty-second Street. I didn't understand what Wall Street was, you know. I thought it was somewhere where all the rich people and celebrities be—that they'd be there just for you to look at. When I got off in New York, I saw the people walkin—it looked like everybody was walkin fast, an the cars was whizzin. I said, "Golly, if I get out there on this street, I'm gonna get hit by one of them cars. It's too crowded in New York!" Then I saw there was two fellas, two Jewish fellas, there to meet me. I had a photograph of them. They told me that I should come with them, that they were there to meet me. While we were walkin down the street, I would look up at the buildins an I ran into a stop-sign. After that I had a stiff neck from lookin up at the buildins.

I got in their car an went out to the agency in Long Island. Leavin the city, I got disappointed. I said, "Oh my God, I just left the country an thought I was comin to the big city, an this man is tryin to send me back to the country!" The man in the agency would tell the people, "I have this nice girl here, she's very attractive, she's eighteen, and she's good with children." You know, they didn't know a thing about you. So they would say, "We'll bring her over in an hour, an when we get there you have to give us one hundred and fifty dollars." I said to myself, "He's sellin the girls. I come all this way just to be bought and sold!"

They took me out to this lady. I remember her well—Mrs. Burke at 250 Central Avenue in Cedarhurst. I got there an looked at this big old apartment building and I said, "It sure is a big old place." I had the idea that she lived there in that big old building all alone, and she expected me to clean it all by myself. I got in there in this little apartment, and she showed me through the rooms. I asked her, "Where do your children live?"

She said, "Here with me."

"Where would I live?"

"Here with me."

"Well, where?"

"You will live and sleep in this room with my children."

"I have to share this room with your children?"

She said, "Yes."

I didn't like it because the little girl slept in a cradle, and I slept in one bed and the little boy slept in the bed with me. I never liked to sleep with anybody. I always slept by myself. Then I had to get used to when the lady would get up early and leave, an you didn't see em no more till five or six or seven o'clock. Then she would come in and have something to eat. She didn't spend time with the children. I would think, she don't love her children, she don't stay home. I wondered why.

I worked there about a month, and I kept askin her, "When is payday, when you goin to pay me?" She said, "Oh, you'll get paid. Do you want me to give you money until you get paid?" So I said, "Yeah." So she gave me money. Her husband took me to Robert Hall's, and I think he bought a coat and two dresses, and shoes. Anyway, I ran out of money, and he came over to the counter, and he asked me did I get everything I wanted, did I have enough money, and did I want anything else. I said no. The lady behind the counter said, "Gee, you got a good boss!"

I said, "Boss?"

And she said, "Do you work for him? Is that your husband?"

"No, I work for him."

"Well, that's your boss."

I said, "Well, I just say it's somebody I work for."

When it came time to get paid, they didn't owe me, I owed them. It came up a big argument. I told her I was supposed to get one hundred and twenty-five dollars a week. She said, "No, I'll show you on the contract." So she went and got this contract, and she showed it to me. We was only supposed to get one hundred dollars a month. I told her to get in touch with this agency. I told her, "I'm from the country, but I got sense enough not to work for one hundred dollars a month. I could stay at home and work for one hundred dollars a month." We called the agency, and the agency had went out of business. She told me that she couldn't afford to pay one hundred and twenty-five dollars a week. She said, "You don't do a lotta cookin." I said, "Yeah, I understand that, but I sits here day and night takin care of your children, takin them to parks. I had to spend my money, cause when I take them to the store they be hollerin about what they want. I didn't want to be embarrassed, so I used my money to buy them things." She offered me forty dollars a week, and I told her I'd try it for a while till I found somethin better.

After that she began to get very nasty and prejudiced. When her company came, she said she didn't want me to sit in the other room and watch TV. I would have to go back into my room until her company left. One day she asked me, "You wasn't used to eatin steak and pork chops in West Virginia, were you?"

I told her, "Yes, I was used to good food in West Virginia."

So she said, "Well, the maids don't get treated like the family."

I said, "Well, I don't know what you mean by 'maid.' A maid is somebody who works in a hotel, right?"

"No, all of you that come up here are maids to us."

So I said, "Oh, you mean that this will be something like slavery time?"

She was from Georgia, and people were still treated like slaves in the Deep South till about 1960. I began to get very angry when she told me her parents had a lotta slaves. Then she said, "I wish it was slavery time, I'd make a good slave out of you!" I got real mad and cursed her. One word followed another word, and then I got so mad that I slapped her, I slapped her hard as I could. I went into the bathroom, and the little boy came into the bathroom and bit me on the leg. I looked at him a long time and then I grabbed him. I started to throw him in the bathtub, but then I thought better of it. So I grabbed him and picked him up, and I turned him upside down by his feet and I started to shake him. Then I just got so mad that I took his head and I put it in the commode.

She asked me was I crazy. I told her no. She said, "Well, you had better go back to West Virginia where they allow you to do that."

I said, "In West Virginia I don't know nothin about no niggers and white and black and all what you talkin about. You got somethin mixed there; you talkin like the deep part of the South. You say 'niggers.'"

She said, "They don't like niggers to hit a white person here! I had a girl from Alabama——"

"Yeah, you had a *girl* from Alabama—they tell me that in the deep part of the South when a nigger gettin ready to spit at them, they put their head in a barrel. But we don't do that in West Virginia."

I got my clothes and went to a friend's house. Later, I called Mrs. Burke and asked her to pay me, and she said she would pay me when I stopped by. I felt a little uneasy goin back, so I asked this guy, one of my friends, to go with me. He went and got his two brothers and said, "Come on, go with me back to get the rest of Rose's things." They were great big guys, six foot four. So I rang the doorbell, and she said, "Who is it?" I said it was Rose. She said, "Well, come on in." I started to open the door, and my boyfriend said, "Let me open it." So he opened the door, and when he opened the door he looked behind the door, and Mr. Burke was standing behind it with a car jack. I guess he was goin to hit me. And her mother, father, and brother was standin there waiting for me. I got my money and the rest of my things, and she tried to talk me into stayin, but I didn't fall for it. I just laughed a lot. I guess it runs in my family, my mother always laughs a lot too. So I got me another job.

I met an old man, he was a chauffeur, and they called him Uncle Dan. He asked me where I worked, and I told him I didn't have no job. He told me that he knew a lady next door to where he was workin where I could get a job. He said that I'd have to tell the lady I was twenty-four. The lady didn't believe me, but she gave me the job. Her name was Miss Walters. She was nice. That's when I learned how to serve big parties, great big parties. It was exciting to work for her, but she was too nosy. One time I went to get my hair fixed, and when I got back, she was up in my room rattlin through my things, but she had got sleepy—she used to have to take pills—so she fell asleep in my bed. She had forgot to put my things back in my drawer, she had took my letters out and was readin them. So I woke her up and asked her, "What you doin rattlin through my things?" She said, "I just wanted to see." I said, "Oh honey, you just wanted to see!" So then I began to play dirty little tricks on her. She lay her rings down, and I took her rings and put them in the sugar dish. I buried the rings in the silver sugar dish they only use for parties, and put it back in the dining room on the thing, and she was looking for it; she thought she had lost it. I guess it must have been about a month or two later, and she was gettin ready to give a big party, and we were cleanin out the sugar dish, and the rings was there. She said, "Oh, good heavens, I wonder how my rings got in there?" I said, "I don't know."

Then I got this job with the Shapiros out near Brookfield Farms. They were Jewish people. Way out on Long Island near Westbury. They were very rich people, but they acted like ordinary people. You know, they wasn't prejudiced or anything. I remember one time their little boy called me black or something. And she go after him, she told him, "Now you shouldn't call her black, cause you go somewhere and they might call you a dirty Jew bastard! Now Rose is whiter than your heels." They were very dark Jews. She told him she wouldn't tolerate nothin like that, she didn't wanna hear nothin like that again.

I think I made eighty dollars a week from her, and she would always give me five or ten dollars extra. She had an Uncle Joe, his name was Judge Greenberg, and he used to come over every Thursday, and when he would leave, he would always leave me a fifty dollar tip. I would call him Mr. Greenberg, and he told told me no, call him Uncle Joe. Her mother told me to call him Grandpa, but I didn't call him Grandpa, I called him Poppa. And I called her Sister. Then she had friends—her sister would come, and her and Uncle Max would always give me ten dollars before they left, and all kinds of bracelets and things.

I got used to bein with them. I was with her to take care of her children, and everywhere she went, I went. They bought me a brand-new car. She used to give me bags and bags of money—she used to trust me to go take it to the bank for her. Before she would pay me, she used to always ask me what was I goin to do with the money. I said, "Oh, go get my hair fixed." I just liked to spend it. So she would take my money and put it in the bank for me—in her bank, you know. Then they stopped giving me my salary—they would put it in the bank for me. What her friends, her mother and her sister gave me, that's what I had to spend. They would buy my clothes. Really, they treated me mostly like I was a daughter. When I started at the Shapiros, I was standin there waitin to clear the table and she said, "You don't eat?" And I said, "Sure I eat. When you finish, I eat." She said, "Oh, no, that don't go in my house. You have to sit down and eat with us." She had a friend come down one time who called me "maid." She said, "Hey maid, give me this!" I turned around and looked at her and rolled my eyes. She said, "Maid, give me a saltine cracker!" She had drank too much. And Mrs. Shapiro told her friend, "Her name is not 'maid,' her name is Rose! I don't have maids!" And she got kinda angry, but then the lady came and told me she was sorry.

Mrs. Shapiro was a terrific woman—I called her silly all the time. Me and her used to get to fightin, we were passin licks. One time she hit me, and I hit her with a mop. The fight happened in the mornin. It was ten minutes to twelve when I came in the night before, and she said it was four o'clock. I said it wasn't, and she said, "You better apologize."

I said, "No!"

She said, "Are you going to apologize?"

"No!"

So she hauled off and slapped me, and I took that mop and hit her across the head with it. Me and her was gittin ready to get it on, and she went runnin upstairs cryin, and Mr. Shapiro come downstairs and asked me what went wrong.

I said, "She hit me."

So he said, "What is she talkin about?"

I said, "When I came in last night she had to get up to open the door."

He said, "That was ten minutes to twelve."

So then she came back and she said, "Rose, I'm sorry."

I said, "All right." So me and her hugged each other and made up.

When the Shapiros took me to Lake Placid, I did a lotta extra work serving parties an different things. I served a party for this lady, at least I thought she wanted me to serve the party, but she wanted somebody to stay upstairs and keep the dog. It was a little red poodle dog. I baby-sat for a little poodle dog, an she paid me twenty-seven dollars. The dog had fainting spells, an they had left a bottle of Scotch there for me to give the dog—half a glass of Scotch and milk. I think the little dog sometime would just fall out to get the Scotch. She kept fainting. Daisy, her name was Daisy. A little French poodle. Daisy kept fainting, an I kept givin Daisy Scotch. So then I decided I'd drink some of the Scotch too. Then after I drank a lot of the Scotch, an Daisy kept fallin out, I gave Daisy a big glass of Scotch. An after I give her that big glass of Scotch and didn't put no milk or anything in it, she didn't faint no more. She didn't faint no more the whole time I was in Lake Placid. She got well. She jus wanted the Scotch.

It was real nice out there with the Shapiros. The only reason I quit, I got pregnant. I met the baby's daddy in a restaurant. I was off and he was off. He paid for my lunch. I told Mrs. Shapiro I had met this nice person, and she was like a mother. When he called to talk to me, she told him that she would like to see him. So he came over, and him and her sit down and talked. After he left, she told me that she thought he was a much older man, too old for me, and she said, "I told him the same thing." She said, "He said he's not married, but honest to God, I believe he is because it seems like I've seen him some place." I come to find out she did know him. He had did some work for her, and his wife was workin for her friend. That's how she found out. But I didn't find out that he was married until I told him that I was pregnant. Then he told me he was married, and he introduced me to his wife. I didn't feel too badly. I said goodbye to him. Then I went home, had my baby, left my baby there in Virginia, and come back and started doin day work. I still visit the Shapiros; they were a nice family. She was a millionaire—she got theaters, oil wells in Texas, theaters upstate, all kinds of land—but to look at her, she looks like jus a old, poor, straight-haired white woman. She's sweet and I enjoyed workin for her. When I stopped workin, I had plenty of money. I had seventeen thousand dollars. And I had all kinds of clothes which she would bring. I didn't never have anything that come from Alexander's or Mays until after I had children. She always bought my clothes from Lord and Taylor's, very expensive clothes. Even underclothes and all. Sometimes I go ride out there on the farm and talk to her, and she still treats me like she always did.

I used to like domestic work, but now I don't. I don't want to clean nobody else's mess up. When you're goin home, they always have to check and look to see have you stole anything. And they always try to give you some kind of old clothes or old furniture instead of payin you. They don't accept nobody as much as they used to. I think everybody now think you be out to get somethin for nothin. I think that's the whole trouble with everything. They think you come into the house to see what they got in the home, then send somebody back to rob em.

I worked for one family and they had a little boy. His parents was prejudiced, and they had to teach him that. He used to always come rub my hand, then he would rub it till he would say, "That don't come off?"

I said, "No, what's it gonna come off for?"

He said, "You mean you black?"

I would tell him, "No, I ain't black, I'm just as white as you. Color's only skin deep."

So he would tell me about this other girl, "Her skin is darker than yours. There was rats in her hair." See, he wasn't talking about rats, he'd be talkin about the curls—you know, how some people got real kinky hair. I told his mother about it, but she just laughed it off. She said, "So what?" I said, "So you must've taught it to him."

I worked for a lady. I went there the first day, and it was cold with snow. I got there and she didn't let me in. She told me that she was takin a shower and to stand outside till she got through takin the shower. I stood out there one hour, and I was so cold. So then she came to the door and looked me up and down. All through her house, everywhere I went, she'd pretend that she was lookin for somethin, but she was really watchin me to see what was I touchin. So then she told me to go walk the dog. She had a little bit of a white poodle named Pepper. I told her, "You know, that's the reason I don't have a dog—cause it seems stupid to me for people to be out there walkin a dog on a leash and waitin for him to go to the bathroom. I don't like that."

She said, "No, no, no, you don't put him on a leash! I want you to wrap him in this blanket and put him in your arms and take him out. Just get some air."

I said, "All right, I don't mind it. I'll do it this time, but don't make it a habit." So I worked for her two days a week. Where I would dust, she would always go over. Even when I would drink out of a glass, drink water, and I had washed out the glass, she would take that glass, put it in her sink, and put Clorox in it. One day we got in an argument. The snow was still on the ground, and she told me to take the dog out.

I told her, "I told you, I don't walk no dog. This dog is not a baby. I do not appreciate takin no damn dog out to walk him in my arms like a baby!"

She said, "I hired you to work for me. You have to do what I pay you for!"

I said, "All right." So I took the dog out in the blanket, and she was hollerin out the door at me. I got so mad with her, I threw the dog down in the snow. She ran out there and got the dog up and jumped in the car and rushed the dog to the doctor sayin the dog probably had caught cold. I told my mother about it, and they got in an argument. My mother told her, "Rose just only threw your dog in the snow, and you rush your dog to the hospital to the doctor. But my daughter's a human being, and she stood out here in the cold and waited on you an hour. And she had a cold, but you didn't even consider that, did you?" She told my mother that I wasn't like her dog, her dog was better. So I never worked for her again. I think she had trouble with a lot of girls.

I married three times, but I just didn't like it. So now I have five children. I have Carmen Giovanni, Donna Jaykita—she's named after a Jewish boy that my mother was workin for, his name was Jay Bruce Mitchell—I have Jonah Leeshawn, then I have Christopher O'Donnell, then I have Jonathan Cleon—a little Jewish boy was named Jonathan, that I was workin for, and I thought it was the prettiest name. I used to get along with all the children I worked for, even the kid who bit my leg. His name was Barry. I used to think he was the sweetest kid. And Stephen, when I worked for the Shapiros, Stephen always wanted to dress up like a girl and act like a girl, and he was eight years old. After he had got ten years old, Stephen always liked for me to bathe him and take him down in my room and put him on my bed and put powder all over him. Then he used to put on my slips, my blouses, my shoes, and my caps—he always used to like to dress up like a girl. I guess Stephen is in his twenties now. He's still a weirdo. He's, you know, a little shaky. I think I worked about five or six places where things were kinda shaky. This one woman told me she was worried about her daughter, what was she to do. I told her, "There ain't nothin you can do. She got to live her own life. You can't tell a person how to live. To each his own. Children don't all times live like the parents want em to live. You have to live with what you feel."

Cecile Waters

Cecile Waters is a self-assured woman who gives the impression of having made the right decisions at important junctures in her life. After the interview I noticed a framed photograph of her son in military dress, a handsome light-complexioned man. "He has all kinds of friends," Cecile commented, "Italians, Jews, Puerto Ricans—they've all been over to the house. Color doesn't matter much to young people today." That appears to be so, but Cecile also made a point of telling me how white employees at a recent job were unable to look her in the eye during the first few days that "Roots" was shown on television.

Cecile is open-minded and ready to adjust to changing times, but she has seen that even the most decent, self-aware people can blunder into painful and irrevocable decisions. So she maintains her optimism, but it is tempered by an alert and discerning intelligence.

My name is Cecile Waters. I was born in a place called Macomus, West Virginia, and I was there until I finished high school. My father was a mail carrier, and he died when I was ten. As you get older the memory leaves, but I remember him. My mother did domestic work. There wasn't anything in West Virginia to do at that time, because, you know, it was segregated, very segregated. At that time it was "colored people"—it wasn't "black people"—and unless you had an education, the only thing that you could do was be a maid, or somethin like that. Where I lived, if you went to a restaurant, it was a cubbyhole for the colored people to stand and eat a hotdog, or have a soda, or whatever—and then the whites would have a comfortable place to sit. This was at Woolworth's and at all the stores. You were born into this, and you didn't know any better. And your parents, they knew better, but there wasn't anything they could do about it either. You just grew up to a hard life, and you really didn't let it bother you that much because you had no choice. You had to live with it.

The schools were segregated, so you didn't have to come in contact with white students. You stayed with your own—which in a way I feel was all right, because after the schools became desegregated, all the activities that we had was completely eliminated. The white students wouldn't go to any integrated dance, and they outnumbered us four to one, so all the proms, and debutante balls, and cotillion, all this was just cut out of the school program. They could still have their thing at the country club, where you couldn't afford to join. And you couldn't fight back because it was their own property. So how could you do anything?

After you left school, there was no work. The men could work on the railroad or in the mines, but not the women. You might get lucky, and maybe you'd be a telephone operator or something like this. That was really a big thing—and there was maybe one or two openings over a period of four or five years. So far as work was concerned, if you didn't work in a hotel, or be a nurse's aide in a hospital, or do domestic work, that was just about it. So after high school I was a steam-tray girl in the hospital. And like I say, everything there was segregated—blacks was on one side of the hospital and white on the other. And the C Floor, that was supposed to be for the very wealthy white people—and if you are light-complected, like I am, you got the special assignment. You know, it's one thing about white people—if you are a fair-skinned Negro or black person, whichever way you want to call it, you are the first ones to get the better job. They don't want trouble, and then they figure by you lookin fair, you're not lookin for trouble either. They just want somethin that looks nicer around them, and they take you. Looks shouldn't have to play a big part, but it does. So I was the one to have to serve the rich white people—I was the right shade. You have to go through all this, plus the darker-colored people would give you a hard time because you were fair. You really didn't have any place to be—you were right in the middle. The blacks didn't want you, and the whites didn't want you either—so you just out there. Everybody gives you a hard time. My father was very fair, and my grandmother—if you saw her you would think she was white. Back there in slavery times you really didn't know how they mixed up the family. The masters, or whatever they called them, would go out and have sex with these women, and naturally the baby was gonna come out black, you know. I'm sure this is how everybody got mixed up. Sometimes, I guess it was for the best—I don't know. Just one of those things.

As the years passed, I worked for so many people that don't know what I am. They say, "Are you Jewish? Are you Italian? Are you black? What are you?"

I says, "Well, I am a person. As long as I get your job done, what difference does it make what I am?"

Sometimes this really gets under your skin. You learn to live with it after awhile, and you just ignore it, because you figure if the person is intelligent enough they are not gonna ask you these questions in the first place. As long as I'm doin your job and you payin me my money for what I am doin—that's all I'm asking for, and I think that's all you should want to know.

After some time at the hospital job, I began doin domestic work for a lady named Mrs. Bretwell. She was more like a motherly type, and she liked me a lot. It was day work—I never had a live-in job, that's a little bit too much. I worked there for more than a year, and then I got married. She gave me my veil and everything for my trousseau. Then, after we got married she said, "Cecile, I always believed that a wife's place is in her home, so I guess now that you are married you better stay home and take care of Frank." So I did. I didn't work anymore.

Well, then my husband got laid off his job with the railroad, and my mother was in New York workin as a chambermaid, so we closed up the house and came to New York to find work. It was such a terrible place, and so different from what I had been used to. It looked like a garbage can, a junkyard. I said, "Well, Frank, no way I could bring up my child here!" And what really knocks you out is to see so many people. Everywhere you go, it was people, people, people. A big change comin from a population of twenty-one thousand to eight million people—a tremendous change, and it takes you a good ten years to really adapt to that type of livin. We moved I guess about six times before we could get in a place we liked and could be comfortable and feel at home. I've always tried to live pretty decent. That's another thing that a lot of white people think—just because you are a domestic worker, they think you live like pigs. You know, they say, "Oh, you look so nice!"—like how can you look so nice comin from where you live? They'd be surprised that a black person could take ten dollars and do as much with it as they can with two hundred dollars. They just don't know how to value money the way we can—we just had to do it because we had no choice.

Around this time I started workin for these psychiatrists. I had a girlfriend that had the job, and she couldn't hold it, so she asked me if I was lookin for work. I said, "Well, I'll go down and see what it's all about."

I met Mrs. Kerwin, and Dr. Kerwin, and they were both psychiatrists. They said, "We would like for you to take the job if you would like it."

So I said, "Well, I'll give it a try."

I started workin for them September 1, and I worked there a good nine years. It was like a trial basis when I started, and then I became like their child's mother and their companion. I had to play the part of the receptionist, the housekeeper, the maid—whatever you want to call it, I was it. And whenever it was in between, you know, then I would go to do all the shopping and take care of the bank business. I was their complete honcho.

Their offices were in their apartment—one on one side, one on the other—and their livin room was their waitin room, so I had to come in contact with the patients. As a matter of fact, I knew them as much as the Kerwins did. Some of them was really kind of eerie, you know. I'm a pretty outgoin person, people always seemed to take to me—and the patients would sometimes come in twenty minutes early so they could talk to me until the time for their appointment. We learned we had a lot in common. The doctors liked that—they wanted it to be like that. They wanted their patients to feel comfortable. That's why they had the office in their home—because they didn't want them to feel unwanted or just like they were only a patient. And if I didn't happen to be in the waitin room—I would be in the back sometimes, and a patient would knock on one of the doors and yell for me—and sometimes I would fix them a soda or whatever, and we would just have a ball. You could tell the difference in the days too—when it was a good day or a bad day—because sometimes they would be sort of close-mouthed, and they would just look out the window overlookin the river. If they kinda drooped their head, you knew that they weren't in that talkin mood.

When I started workin for the Kerwins, all of that was new to me. In the first place, a psychiatrist was—we thought in terms of a person bein completely crazy. So when you get there and you see that people have therapy and they are not crazy—that's a lesson in itself. Everybody could use some therapy. As a matter of fact, it's the best thing in the world if you can afford it, because then you don't have so much to back up in your mind. A lot of people would talk to a psychiatrist, but they wouldn't talk to anybody else. So like I say, I met so many different types of people while I was there. I didn't have a college education, but that's an education in itself. Experience is the best teacher in the world, and you'd be surprised how much you can learn if you just observe. We used to have some patients, one man in particular, that would yell and scream—and they would be just lookin like you when they went in, and then they would yell all of a sudden, and they would scream and beat, and they would do this and that. This man was about two hundred twenty-five pounds and sometimes I would just tell myself, "Let me lay this knife over here on the side just in case somebody come through here who's really off their rocker." He would scare me just that bad. And after he come out of the office, he would wipe his eyes and go in the bathroom and wash his face and straighten up—like nothin had happened. You'd think from the sounds in the office that this person would run out the door in a rage, but he'd be just as calm as when he went in. I would ask Dr. Kerwin, "Aren't you afraid of those men when they do all of this?"

And he said, "No, it's just gettin all that out that they want to come out, and this is the way they reacted."

It's really an experience. There was so much that I saw that was incredible. They would have these group-therapy classes that would go on sometimes the whole weekend. They would put mattresses and pillows on the floor—and I don't know if you watched it on TV, but one time I was watchin a story about a guy on dope, and they was gettin it out of him, and he was beatin the floor—well a lot of that happens in those group therapies also. They'd be beatin and hollerin and cryin—and the group would be sayin, "Get it out! Get it out!" And you don't know whether to run or to stand there. If they wanted to take off their clothes and come struttin through nude—you standin up there with your mouth open, not knowin what to think—they didn't think it was nothin, you know. You just had to go ahead and not pay any attention to it either—you say, "Well, I guess they need to be doin it." There was no modesty, no pride, no nothin. It was just like—"Well, you never seen a nude person? I'm nude, and that's that!" But anyway, like I say, it was a lot of experience and it was good. You would gradually get into these things, because bein there year after year you would gradually work into it yourself. You knew what to expect, and you knew what was happenin. When they got hungry, I would serve sandwiches. They would stop what they were doin—all this yellin and screamin—and I'd serve. It was just like the whole thing had changed from night to day. And then they'd go back in, and it started up again.

Then I was there durin the time they did this yoga meditation. They would have groups to come in there to do this. Well, you thought they was crazy if you were to see the different motions, everything they went through, what they would eat, and all this kind of stuff. It really was crazy, but again, after they come out of that they would get up and put on their clothes and go about their business just like anything else. It takes all kinds of people to make a world, so you just accepted them for what they were. The experience was great that I got there. With Dr. and Mrs. Kerwin bein as open as they were, it was easy to ask questions. No matter what it was, you didn't feel cramped at all. It was just like talkin to my brother or sister or somethin. Even now, I help other people by what I learned there. There's been a lot of people that had problems and things, and I would sit down and talk with them—and you'd be surprised that they just depend totally on me to give them advice on whatever they should do.

Then in the middle of all this—I'd been there six years when Mrs. Kerwin had to have an operation. She said, "Cecile, I have to go to the doctor, and I don't feel good about it. I don't know how I'm gonna feel when I come back."

So I said, "Well, you don't know, you can't predict your own case. Just go ahead and see what's wrong. You might be just fine."

When she came back she said, "Well, Cecile, it was just like I thought—

I have a cyst on my ovary, and I have to have an operation. I had one before, and I know what I have to go through."

I said, "That's even better—now you know it's not gonna be too much."

So finally she said, "Well, I think so too."

The day that she was comin out of the hospital, I asked Dr. Kerwin, "When are you gonna pick her up?"

He said, "I have somebody that is gonna do it." It was one of his patients—a man who was twenty-six years old.

This man brought Mrs. Kerwin back, and she come in and says, "Cecile, I'm not gonna be in my bedroom, I'm gonna stay in my office."

"Yes," I said, "you mean you're gonna stay in your office while you're recuperatin?"

And she said, "Yes, but I have to talk to you about somethin later."

And just as soon as she and that young man went in that office, they became lovers. If they'd been lovers before, nobody knew it.

So a couple of days later she says to me, "Cecile, I want to talk to you about what's happenin, because I feel you need to know."

I says, "Yes, I sure do, because I don't know what's happenin now!"

I knew that this patient was Dr. Kerwin's patient—and both of the Kerwins were so nice and so understandin that you would never think that anything like this would be goin on. So then I asked him, "Well, what's goin on?"

He said, "We are gonna talk to you about it."

So we go in, and we sit down and talk, and she told me that they were gonna separate, and Stanley was gonna get his own office someplace. And I said, "What is the reason for this?"

She said, "You know Mark has been around here—this is why we are separatin."

"For Mark?" I said. "You got to be kiddin!"

Well, of course, I was shocked to death. I mean, I've heard of things like this happenin, but I never thought I'd see it. Mrs. Kerwin was at least twenty-five years older than this boy—but it got stronger and stronger every day. So finally, Dr. Kerwin found his apartment, and then I was goin back and forth to his place down the street. And then this Mark moved in with her. It was such a pathetic case.

In the meantime, their adopted daughter is there. Adele is already confused, because when she was six years old her parents told her she was adopted. The Kerwins never wanted her to know, but then Adele's cousin found out from her mother—and they didn't want Adele to hear all this from another child, so they had to explain to her that she was adopted. By the time I get there Monday, Adele is a wreck. She just didn't know what to do or what to think or anything. She couldn't believe that she was adopted. She was mad and angry—she was hurt, and she just let them know how she felt. So then she clinged to me that much more, because she just felt like I was more her mother—and she was hostile to em for a long time. They didn't know how to explain the adoption to that child, because they were just babies too, you know.

I took care of Adele as if she was mine. I felt this way—this was just the way I felt. I don't think I could have loved my own child no more than I did her—and I still feel that way about her. I think that was why we had such a good relationship—because I didn't look at it like she was somebody else's. I brought Adele to my house a couple of times—as a matter of fact, quite a few times. She would call me "Cessie," because she couldn't say "Cecile" when she was young. I fed her; I kept her. She spent the night with me and everything. I guess bein away from home was a little bit strange, and whenever I would take her to my mother's or somethin like that, she was right up under me all the time. But otherwise, she got along fine. It opens them up when they see that it's not much different where I live. Now Adele's thirteen, and she is still confused. Her readin abilities and things that she is supposed to be doin for her age—she still can't do it. It's an emotional problem. You know, bein a psychiatrist, you would think that they would have handled it different—but I guess when somethin is yours, you think that you know it all, you know you got all the answers.

Mrs. Kerwin and Mark were together for about two and a half years, and I understand he went on about his business. In 1973 Mrs. Kerwin told me she only needed me part-time, so I found another job. We keep in touch all the time—I spoke to them last week. If I need anything, I can still go and say, "Dr. Kerwin, I need a hundred dollars"—and he would just reach in his pocket and give it to me. Of course, I would pay it back, but, you know, this is the friendly terms that we are on.

My last job was as a showroom manager—plannin executive lunches and things like that. It was a good-sized company, but they only had about six or seven blacks workin there—the minimum the law required. Now, you know, when "Roots" was on, I think it kind of upset everybody in the beginnin. It was about the third night before I would watch it all the way through—it was so brutal. This is the part that hurt—when you know you had people that had to go through this. Durin that week, I'd come in to watch and they'd all turn away from me and look at each other. So then one night after work one girl asked me, "Cecile, are you watchin 'Roots'?"

I said, "In the beginning I couldn't watch it, but now I'm watchin it."

"Well, what do you think about it?"

I says, "Well, there's good and bad in all of it. At least it's somethin we can all learn from. Naturally, it is goin to upset you when you first look at it, because you just can't see how people could have treated anybody this way—a human bein—no matter who it is. But I guess you have to throw that part out of your mind and think about how far you have come and how much better off you are now, and be grateful. I think in the future, maybe all of this will pass over, and people will become one."

I guess it had to happen—at least it did happen. I believe in acceptin things for what is, and not wishful thinkin. I'm not a genius, so I can't wish I was a genius—you know what I mean? I'm secure bein who I am—I think I have a pretty healthy mind. I just take things in stride—if you like me, okay, and if not, then I'll just maybe crack a joke with you and leave it at that.

Lu Anne Jones

I MET LU ANNE JONES WHEN I WENT TO INTERVIEW LAURA LEE JONES, HER mother. I enjoyed talking with Laura Lee, but she remained cautious and never really gave a candid account of her work experience. Lu Anne, though, was anxious to talk. She was sixteen at the time and a little nervous at first. "Tell him about the snake," Laura Lee prompted, and Lu Anne dutifully launched into a recitation of that childhood adventure. At first she looked to her mother for support, like a child trying to remember her lines in a grade-school play, but after this initial anecdote, Laura Lee merely listened, leaving Lu Anne room to assert her own distinct view of things. I was moved by the mother's tactful restraint. Even when Lu Anne criticized employers for whom her mother had worked uncomplainingly for years, Laura Lee maintained her attentive silence. And when Lu Anne exclaimed, "God, this is stupid! We had to clean up everybody's house when we was slaves. Didn't they get enough of bein slaves?" Laura Lee's composure remained unchanged. Lu Anne's angry words seemed far removed from the entertaining storytelling of her mother, but after awhile I began to feel that her narrative revealed attitudes her mother felt but left unspoken—thoughts she had to keep from her consciousness in order to perform her domestic chores. It is an oversimplification to say that Lu Anne expressed what her mother concealed, but I felt a strong bond of understanding between the two women.

Lu Anne's life has not been easy, and the coming years will continue to test her. No wonder she enjoys "I Dream of Jeannie," the television series in which a servant, a woman, manipulates the world around her with magic power. It is a congenial fantasy for the daughter of a household worker, a brief respite from the difficult challenges that lie ahead.

I'm Lu Anne Jones. I'm sixteen. I was born in South Carolina. I still can remember when I was real small, when I lived down South with my grandmother. My mother was living up North because she had to make some money to take care of us. They was makin little money down there, not enough to take care of Grandma too. I didn't like it in the South; I was very lonesome. There was a railroad track—there was kids across the railroad track, nicknamed Momma, and we always used to go play with them. One day when we was playin I saw her dog—he was on the railroad tracks and the train ranned over him. Cut him up in all pieces. So we had to take him up and put him in a box and take him to the woods and bury him.

One time I seen this snake. You know the way them old-fashioned stoves is made with the big pipe to let the smoke out, well anyway I was in the kitchen and I looked up and the snake was starin at me, lookin me in the eye. I went and got my Uncle Willie. He was sittin there on the porch puttin on his boots. So he went and got his shotgun. Then he went and got the boys across the street and they came over and shot the snake, but they didn't kill it. It went down in the house. So they had to go get a ax, and then they killed him and put him on the railroad tracks.

As I was growin up my mother had married my stepfather. My real father got poisoned up North. He was about twenty-two when he died, and I was just a little kid. I never seen him—I seen him on a picture. They say I look just like him and that I should've been a boy.

I was around six when I moved North. My mother came down to fetch me. I was kind of sad for leavin my grandmother, but I had to go. We came up by train. I was pretty excited. I moved to Great Neck—Nana's house. This lady was keepin me. My mother paid her, but she gave us oatmeal three times a day. We used to get oatmeal all the time. We didn't have decent food and stuff. We just went outside and played most of the time. Nana's husband, her daughter, and her son lived there. Her son used to take his sister to the park, but he never took us. It was just a business for Nana.

I stayed at Nana's a few weeks. Then my mother and stepfather brought me to Roslyn. I felt better. Sometimes I felt ashamed because like in Roslyn you'd see winos and stuff runnin around the streets and beggin for money, but if you go in the white folks' neighborhood you don't see that—it's clean. The black section, it's all dirty and stuff. So I was wonderin why the black have moved up like that. The whites, if they see one bad, they use it on all of em. Then they say, "Black no good, blacks do this, blacks nasty and stuff." I visited some white houses. I used to work with my mother. I remember my first visit to Mrs. Gutman. Momma used to always dress us nice—she used to put out our clothes for us to wear. We used to go there and she'd fix us somethin to eat. And we'd sit

in the back, me and my sister, in the backyard and eat. And Mrs. Gutman had this little dog named Caesar; he's dead now, he was a good little thing, and we used to play with him. We used to sit out there and relax, and my mother would come out there and say, "Want any more to drink?" And Mrs. Gutman, she'd fix us food and stuff. She was nice to us.

Sometimes I'd look at Mrs. Gutman's face and say to my sister, "Ooo, how pale she looks!" Sometimes I'd be wonderin, why is it white people get suntans and it hurts, and when black people do it it don't hurt? I always felt I had to behave special. I used to have to say, "Yes" and "No"—I'd say it anyway, I wouldn't say "Yes, ma'am," I'm not like that—but I'd say it in a softer voice. When I said hello to her, I'd blush. When I helped my mother, sometimes I'd vacuum the rooms up. My mother would come and check behind me. The house was real nice—the floors clean and stuff like that. I wished I had their color TV. Now, you know, since I got bigger I just say, "What's the difference between a color one and a black-and-white one?"

You know, sometimes when the white people come in, and their friends come in, I felt embarrassed cause I'm workin in the house. And I say, "Wow, God, we're slaves again!" I'm lookin at em and they're starin. Sometimes Mrs. Gutman would bring me out to meet her guests. I'd just take it, say thank you and then forget it.

On Christmas I used to always get presents from the Gutmans. They'd give me jewelry or a little perfume.

When I cleaned I used to always look for quarters and money. That'd be my own secret.

They had a son David. He was a few years older. Sometimes he used to stay and play with us, play games, cause he had a lot of games. It seemed funny to come back home from the Gutman house. I was wonderin, "How come they're so rich, so wealthy, and the black people don't have what the white people have?" I guess I thought that's the way the world is.

After Mrs. Gutman I helped my mother at Mrs. Lewin's. I did the same as I used to do at Mrs. Gutman's house. I'd clean the bathroom and stuff. Her husband would give me money, like a dollar, two dollars. They were nice too, but I couldn't be myself; I had to be extra special.

We had a room in a black neighborhood, just two rooms for my mother, my stepfather, me, and my little sister Tina. My mother had the big bedroom and Tina and I had the small room. We shared a kitchen with another family. The building was messed up. The water dripped in the bathroom. An old lady owned the building. She used to go around chewing snuff and spittin it out, and when she talked you could see all of it in her mouth. The floors were fallin apart, steps and stuff. It was an old raggedy house just next to the white folks' neighborhood. It made me wonder how come they're so rich and me out there in this poor neighborhood. It wasn't really poor, but it didn't look like the white people's houses out there.

My mother worked really hard, you know, and what makes me so mad, when she gets through they ask her, "Laura, did you clean up the bathroom?" It makes me so mad. Then I say to myself, "No wonder they can

stay so healthy, because they don't do nothin. All they do is sit down and watch TV. Or eat or somethin like that. Then they have a maid come in their house and clean it up." It would make me mad to see them so lazy not to clean up their own house. When I was workin out here for this lady, she only had a small apartment, just one kid and her husband, and she couldn't clean it up herself. She used to pay me five dollars for four hours. She used to ask me to do things like clean the stove and mop the kitchen and clean out the bathroom. I used to take my time. I used to say, "Why work hard for just five little dollars?" So I used to take my time and wait till eight o'clock come. Then she'd say, "Can you stay longer?" And I said, "No, I have to go home now." She ain't gonna overwork me for no five dollars! If I'da stayed, betcha she would of paid me five dollars and then let me clean up the whole house. They was lazy, so lazy. I felt proud I wasn't lazy, but I wasn't very proud workin in a house. You know I can understand why my mother would do it, because as she was comin up she couldn't go to school. She had to work on the farm and stuff. She had a little bit of learnin, but not that much for her to get a really good job. But as for me, I'm gonna finish school and then go on to college after that, and I'm not gonna be slavin in no white people's house with all the learnin I'm gonna have. That wouldn't make any kinda sense. I wouldn't want to clean up any white person's house. Why don't they clean it up theirself? I just look at some of these colored people cleanin up white people's houses, and I say, God, this is stupid! We had to clean up everybody's house when we was slaves. Didn't they get enough of bein slaves?"

When I came to Westbury, that's when I really found out that the blacks couldn't stand the whites, and stuff like that. When I went to junior high the blacks used to pick fights with the whites. And we used to see movies in Health Class—we had a black teacher in Health—and he used to tell us how white people used to treat the black, and stuff like that. So we'd be seein movies and stuff, you know, like slaves, how they beat up slaves. They treated em so bad. We saw a Martin Luther King picture when he was a little boy and comin up with the slaves. He used to be a slave. They used to beat him and beat him and make him get on the back of the bus and let the whites sit in the front. You know, that made the kids more angry, and they'd start fights and stuff with the whites and call em all kinds of nasty names.

I had one nice white teacher. He was white mixed with Indian. He was very nice. You know, we didn't have to do any work. He was so nice. And like he used to take us out for lunch and stuff and take pictures of us and we used to go on picnics. He used to play around with us just like a black person. We could say anything in front of his face we wanted. When the other kids were in class working, he'd take us out and we'd go outside and play kickball and listen to records. But like, he wouldn't play no white people's records, he'd be playing black music. So we was really close.

We didn't speak to the white kids, but like, if the black kids wanted money off em, they'd say, "Give me your money, if you don't, I'll beat you up!" And they'd just hand over their money. You know, I used to do it too. We used to go up to em and say, "You got a quarter?" If they'd say no, we'd search their pockets and take it. But it got so bad that kids were tellin the principal, so that if any kid asks any other kid for money and take it, they get suspended for a day. I still do it sometimes, but most of the time now my mother gives me a dollar a day, cause now she can afford it. Sometime some whites are nice, but some of em are snotty. But like if I do it now, I jus say, "Give me a quarter!" and if they don't give it to me, I jus say, "Well, I'm goin to beat your butt!" I jus feel anger because I can't stand em anyway.

I had white friends; they wasn't really my friends though. They'd listen to me, but I didn't want to be the boss. Like anything I'd say, they did it. But sometimes I don't feel right havin people just jump to what I say. There's no sense in bein friends if they are scared of me. Sometimes I jus think, well, why should they be scared of me? I'm not goin to bother them or nothin cause I'm black and they're white. Sometimes, I see the white people and the black people be playin around in school and my friends say, "Now, jus look at that, aren't they stupid?" Then we call them honkies—that's another name for white people. We would say, "Hey, look at that honky over there playin with the black!" Then we see some of the black families with the whites, we jus call them honkies too, cause they're in with the whites.

Some white people, they're real snotty; they can't stand blacks. I've seen white people and black mixin and having kids. So I just say, "God, that kid's gonna look mighty funny." He's gonna look funny, right? If you see a little mixed kid, you know people make fun of him. So I say, "God, you know he gonna have a hard time in the world! If the world doesn't change, he's gonna have a hard time, because he's mixed—he sees a black father and a white mother." When I see that, I can't stand it. I say, "Look at that black fool! You know, it's stupid to mix up with a white person."

Sometimes I think I'm tougher about race than my mother; sometimes she is. She don't dislike the whites or nothin like this, but sometimes she thinks about way times back, bout what happened, and jus takes it out on the whites. Like if somethin happened, right, if a white lady hit a colored person, they'd call all kinds names—"You white this; you white that!" Jus bringin out your natural feelings, you know, everything you hate inside. Jus bring them right out and tellin it. I remember one time me and my sister were at the Westbury Library, and this white girl, she had made a funny face at my sister. I have a bad sister, and she didn't like it, so she started cussin up the white girl and they was gonna fight. So after I came in I said, "If you fight my sister, you gonna have to fight me!" So she jus dropped the subject and went into the library to her friends. They said, "What did we do; we didn't do anything to your sister." My sister said, "Well, your friend was makin a face at me." So then they had went into the library—we took all the air out of their tires. Then she called her father, and there was the father chasin after us in the car. They couldn't catch us. Then I thought they had caught my sister, so I went back to look for her, and she was in a white peoples' garden pickin tomatoes and eatin em. My sister loved tomatoes, and when she seen em she picked em. Then the white man saw us and he said, "You act like black monkeys climbin up a tree!" So we said, "Your mother!" and jus kept on goin.

Tina is really nice. Me and her used to go out and stuff, but then she started hangin round with the wrong people; they'd get her messed up. I'd tell her not to hang around with them, but she started gettin into trouble and she had to go to court a lot of times. She never really got in any serious trouble like breakin in and robbin people's houses, jus stayin out late at night. She went to court and stuff; then she got put in the home; then she came out, did the same thing over again—in the home, came out, over again, in the home again. My mother tried to help. Tina's still my buddy, I don't care how she does, she's my sister. I don't blame anyone for what she did, it was her own mistake. But, you know, these older mens around forty, they really should be shamed of theirself because they shouldn't mess around with younger kids. Tina is fifteen now. Since she's gone, it's lonesome in the house with nobody to play cards with.

Sometimes I watch TV and I see "I Dream of Jeannie." I see her on TV and I say, "God, I wish I could be like her!" Then I think to myself, "I wonder if anybody in this world is really magic, can do wonderful things like go pop and make big houses and stuff? I wish I could do that." If I get married I don't wanta work. I jus wanta sit down and take care of the kids.

I had my baby with this English dude. He was colored. His folks came from Jamaica. He was really nice. We was plannin to get married, but I said no. I had one more year of school, so I quit him. The man I'm goin with now, he's a Natty Dread—they have a religion, they don't tell no lies; when they wash their hair, they don't pick it out or nothin. They don't cut their hair; they braid it. I'm gonna have a wealthy husband—let him go out and work and I stay home. And I wanta have anything I want. If I'm home all day, no sense to me havin a housekeeper, but if I ever have one it's gonna be a white one cause I'm gonna get back at em. I'm not sayin that jus to say it, but I think of that sometimes.

I want my daughter Mora to have a lot of things. I want her to learn karate so she can take up for herself in case anybody tries to bother her. If she gets in a fight she'll know how to defend herself. But I'm hopin she'll never get in any fights. I want her to learn how to play the drums and how to sing.

I would want Mora to know everything that I know about history, like how the whites treated us and how we didn't have equal rights to vote. I'd say, "If the whites be nice to you, be nice to them, but if they're not nice to you, forget em."

I guess the whites think, "Well, we was the head leaders way back, so we still the head leaders now." They still tryin to get us to be slaves again, but, you know, they jus can't make it because they don't have that much power. Nobody ain't gonna make me no slave. They still think, "Since we have money, they're our slaves, we'll tell them what to do!" Forget it! They don't boss me. My mother—that's the only person that can boss me, my mother. But if some white people come up and try to boss me—they'll never get over.

Laetitia Mackey

There wasn't much left of Laetitia Mackey's block. It had probably been a pleasant neighborhood twenty-five years ago—large, healthy trees lined the street, and the two-story row houses with their tiny front yards looked rather charming as I approached. But the street was empty. No cars. No children. Empty yards. Doors and windows sealed by bolted metal plates. Laetitia had told me her home had a blue door. It was not hard to find; it was the only door left.

Laetitia was nervous when we began the interview and made some slight factual error that bothered her. I told her this was no problem, that I could correct it when I transcribed the interview, but she insisted that we erase the tape and start over. Laetitia wanted her story to be accurate, and even though I'd promised to correct her unimportant slip, she simply could not bear the thought of having her narrative begin with a moment of confusion. The incident brought home to me just how important it was for Laetitia and many of the other women to have this chance to record their personal experiences—"to leave a footprint in the sand here," as Eva McQuay puts it in her interview.

On our second attempt, Laetitia relaxed, and her story came out so readily, so energetically, that I was practically a spectator. At times Laetitia shot out of her chair to give dramatic renditions of incidents in her past. Her strongest performances were reserved for her most unpleasant memories: her first days in New York; sexual come-ons from white men; the languid bossiness of her most spoiled employers. Her imitations were cruel, persuasive, and quite wonderful: the frenzied activity of New York streets; the ugly, threatening swagger of the white man who assumed she was his for the asking; the tranquilized suburban matron who could not quite bring herself to answer her own phone. The special intensity of these impromptu performances came from a reserve of anger and anxiety that had not been lost in time. There is no way a mere transcription can capture the tenor of all that, so I was particularly anxious to at least get some good photographs of Laetitia to accompany her narrative. I went back a few months later; the place seemed more desolate than before. And when I came to Laetitia's door, I found it had been sealed shut.

*M*y name is Laetitia Mackey. I am thirty-nine years old. I was born the fourteenth of December, 1936, in a little small town called Fayetteville, North Carolina. Comin up as a child, I can remember us living in about a seven-room white house on the Merkson Road. My mother, she was a domestic worker. She worked in people's homes taking care of children and housekeepin. She had to take care of all the bills and everything because our father had separated from us. She never received welfare checks; she always believed in goin out and workin and tryin to take care of us herself. And I remember she would often tell us, "I don't know how I am goin to make it, children, but by the help of the Lord we will make it." And she would go out, and she would earn something like ten dollars or twelve dollars weekly, and we had to live off of this. She would have to go out to work and leave us—and as me bein the oldest child at the home, I had a lot of work to do in the house. My mother would always tell me that I had to clean the house, and I had to cook if necessary. So I was only about the age of nine years old when I started to learn about housekeepin.

Ever since I can remember, my mother worked for white families, but she never discussed with me about the hard times or nothin goin on with the jobs. I was only a little girl; I can't remember so much about those times. The only thing that I knew—she used to come in the house, and she'd be tellin us, "Oh, the day was so hard! I had so much work to do, and I have to come home, and I have to do lots of things. You children have to help me out." That's about as much as I knew; that's all she would discuss with us. She would never really—I think my mother really didn't want us to know just how hard times was. But, you know, by lookin on and observin you could see the expression on her face; you could tell when times come that wasn't so good. She would go in the kitchen, and she would start hummin and singin and carryin on. As a child along the time that I grew up, there wasn't so much that you could say to your parents. They would say, "Oh, girl, you go in there and sit down. Don't bother me, I'm tired." You know, they never really discussed some things with you, like hard times.

I never went on the job with my mother. She used to work for this family—they had children growin up like me and my brother—and they would give my mother shoes and clothin for me and such things as that. When I was quite small, I didn't know no difference, but as I became to be a teen-ager I didn't like it because I wanted new clothes. My mother would bring things home, and I knew that she'd gotten them from someplace that she was workin. I didn't want to wear them, cause like in school the kids would say, "Ugh, your mother let you wear hand-me-down clothes." And sometimes the kids in school would laugh at you.

We was the type of children that had to go to church on Sunday, and through the week we went to school every day. And when we come back home we had an obligation in the house to do, so we did not have the time to be runnin around out there in the street to find out what was really goin on out there. Our time was really occupied in the home. We really lived in a separate world.

I met my husband when I was livin in Fayetteville. We had an army base there which is called Fort Bragg. I was walkin down the street and he was standin with some G.I.s at the corner—myself and a couple of girlfriends was walkin, and so the guys started talkin, and so we just made a conversation, and he asked me if he could make a date with me. I hesitated, and we gossiped for awhile. So I told him he could come back Saturday afternoon. My mother didn't really approve of it. I started thinkin about growin up and how you don't get things that you want, and I said, "Well, I met this guy, a G.I., and I know he have money, and he can maybe give you money sometimes and help me out with, you know, if it might be somethin I wanted, he would get it for me." So we dated for about four months, and then we got married.

For five years we was very happy together, but then my husband—I really hate to say this—we started havin trouble in the home. He started goin outside, and he found somethin outside better than what he had in his home—or he thought he did. After that we separated and I come up to New York.

Believe me, I was here one week and I was ready to go back. Growin up, I had heard a lot about the big city, and I had heard a lot about the bright lights—and when I came and I saw all the tall buildings and saw all the people movin in the streets, I said, "Who in the world could live in a place like this with the peoples in the street? They's pushin each other; it's overcrowded, and everybody's in a hurry. Nobody have time to even speak to each other. How in the world can peoples live in a place like this?" And I was ready to go back home. I was livin with my brother and his wife. They was livin here about five years before I came to New York. So, my sister-in-law, she used to tell me, "Laetitia," she said, "you realize you never been in the city before, and the city is much different from just where you come from. You come from the South and you never seen a lot of people all in one place together like this. But if you stay here awhile, you will like it. And you will make some money, and you get your own little bank account started, and you find out that you don't have to be in a distress for money. You'll have money to spend, and you'll have money to save, and you will like it then. The reason why people don't speak to you when you walkin—they don't have time for that. Like where you come from in North Carolina, there's not as many people as there are in this place—the people that you see back home is a space apart. But here like, the peoples is all together, there's so many people everywhere, and people be rushin to jobs, and people be rushin home.

Their work hours is different; some people be goin to work at different times, and nobody don't have time on the street to be speakin and stoppin and holdin conversation with each other. There is a lot of difference in this place than in the place where you came from."

When my kids came here they got adjusted right away; they didn't even have to go through no struggles or hard times. They started school the third day they was in New York. They caught on to everything much faster than I did. It was nothin with my children as it was with me. When I came, I was very lonely, and it seemed like I couldn't get adjusted to the people. The way that the people lived here was altogether different from the way I was raised, and the things that I could see bein done in the streets and things that was bein done in the home, it was very much different. It was just like, well, it was nothin that was bad, it was just the way everybody would be. Even in the house people were rushin around, just rushin around, and I could not understand it. Like when they would get ready to cook a meal, they just get the food together and they put it on the stove, and they have this ready in five minutes, and they have that in five minutes—it was just a whole new life for me. Even when I came into my sister-in-law's house, and she would be like—I got to do this and I have got to do that—and she would be lookin at the clock every five minutes. I got to do this, I got to go to the hospital, I have to go to Broadway, and I have to do this. Everything was did in a certain length of time. It was just like, "I got to get this out of the way or else." Everything was happenin so fast, so fast, and I was never used to anything like that growin up in North Carolina. Then after I came to know how everything was movin in the city, I started movin fast like everything else.

My first job in New York, I was a chambermaid doin household work at the St. George Hotel in Brooklyn. As long as I worked in the hotel, the management of the hotel was great. Dealin with the guests, that's where the little run-ins would come in. A couple of times, more than a couple of times, I would go to make up a room where there is only one man checked in there. As a routine, the customer occupyin the room is supposed to be out to let the maid make the room up. A couple of times when I'd go to the room the door would be unlocked—I'd go in and the man would be closed up in the bathroom, and he would be quiet in there. I would open the door and he would say, "Come in, don't you like to make some fast money?" He'd be nude. I got very angry, very angry, and I would run out of the room and go to the nearest telephone that was on the floor and call the desk and say, "The man in such-and-such a room, he's in the nude in the hotel; he's givin me a hard time, and I refuse to make this room up because he's not supposed to be in the room while I am making it up. Now this man is up there and he's tellin me to come in the bathroom with him, and he wants to show me a good time, and he's offerin me money, and I don't like to be goin through stages like this because it's very terrible and embarrassin." Several times this happened. I have even had the experience of men layin in bed. You knock on the door and they won't answer the door, so you take it for granted nobody's in the room. You go in the room to make it up and you find him layin in the bed in the nude, and he's talkin about, "Put off your clothes and let me look at you"—all these kind of things—"I want to get a kick, and I will give you fifty dollars to do this and fifty dollars to do that." You know, it was quite a experience. It was a very terrible embarrassment— some of the things, you wouldn't even want to approach nobody tellin them about it. You try to get out of the room as fast as you can; you go down and make complaints. What can you do? These things happen livin in a hotel.

I think it made a difference I was black—the way they would approach you, you know. They figure, like, well it seems that they wouldn't come out in words, but the way they would approach you and the way they look at you. You could read them, that they think, "Well, how much money can you be makin for a job like this? I know that you will like to make extra money. You can't be makin but so much, and nobody would never know about this but me and you. I can get over fast with you. What can you make in a day? How much money can you make in a day doin work like this? Where are you from?" All these kinds of things. It is not so much the words, but the way they would approach you with certain phrases that they would use talkin to you. What they would ask you would pretty much let you know that they were the sort who look at the color you are, too. Most of the white men, they would try to talk to you in a hip tone of voice. They would try to maybe tell you about three or four things while you are thinkin about one thing. They are steady rappin, you know—"I would like a black woman. They tell me a black woman is good." I have heard things said like that. And not only on the job. I have heard these things said to me out in the streets quite a few times in Manhattan. Yeah, quite a few times. I couldn't hardly walk any place by myself. I have had white guys follow me in the streets and approach me with words sayin, "Hey baby, let's get over. With that fine figure you got, you look like you could really make a man happy." All those kind of things. This attacks my respect. I have had a couple of times, had guys try to attack me—white men. I remember one time on Broadway, I was just comin up out of the subway. I have really had more experiences in this place than I can speak of. I was just comin out of the subway, Nassau and Broadway subway stop, and I was comin out to the street headin towards Court Street. As I was almost at the corner of Court Street this white guy bumped into me and he grabbed my waist. He grabbed me, he said, "Hey, come on, you goin with me, with your black beautiful self! They tell me all bitches like you"—I mean, this is the word, I'll never forget this, he said, "They tell me all the bitches like you is good."

I said, "Hey man, get your hands off me! Don't touch me!"

"I want to touch you. I'm going to get your body. Come, you and me's goin to the hotel."

"I'm not goin any place with you! You don't know nothin about me, and I knows nothin about you. Get your hands off me cause I'll holler, and I will holler for the policeman right now if you put your hands on me again." And so he grabbed me round the neck and he started like to pull me off the street into a store entrance. I kicked him, and by me kickin him he had to let go, and I ran around the corner.

Now the way I feel about white people, I don't hate them or nothin, but I do have a little discrimination against them because, you know, it seems like they only class all the black people as one way. It seems that they never realize that there is a difference in the black nationality of people as well as any other race of people. There is some good blacks, there are some bad blacks, and there are some middle-class blacks, and some common blacks, and there is some really up-to-date blacks—but it seems like the white man only class black peoples as one race. And it seems like as a black woman walking into the street, the white man only looks at her one way—that she is just black trash, she is nothing, and I can do anything to her that I want to and I can get over. I mean, they won't prosecute me in court cause who is she—she is black, and I don't have to go through no hassle, no charges, with her. And so I can get what I want from her, and I don't have to worry about bein prosecuted for it. It seems that they have these things built up in their minds. But I don't correspond with that because I don't compare myself with other blacks. As I said, there is some blacks that are low-class blacks and they don't care what they do. Other blacks, they have a fear, they have so much of a fear towards the white man because they know that all down through the years, growin up, as far back as they can remember, they have always been under the white man's control. Basically everything that they have, even though they go and buy it out of a black man's store, most of what this black man got in his store, when it comes down to the real facts of where is came from in the beginning, is still coming from the white man. It just makes the black man or woman know that they don't have the equal rights with the white people. As far as I'm concerned with the white man or the white woman, when I do out there and I do a day's work for them, I just do my work. As far as I am concerned, they don't love me and I cannot love them because I know that there is a space difference, there is a racial gap, because that white woman or white man that you go and work for in their home, when the time comes for them to serve dinner, they will not let you sit down at that dinner table and eat with them. They will tell you, "Serve us, Laetitia, and then after you serve us you can have your dinner in the kitchen"—where you do the cookin, not in the dining room where they sit down and eat their dinner themselves. So you know when things like this happen there is a complex racial gap somewhere.

Housework is where you really have the problems. The first time I entered a white home to do housework was in Queens, Long Island. I was working for this lady; she was Jewish. She had two children—the little girl was in kindergarten and the son in the second grade. When I first went there she was tellin me so many things to do, I said, "It's impossible. Now how can I do all these things?" I worked there for a couple of days, and I was really tryin to do everything this woman was tellin me to do. I had to be up seven o'clock in the morning and I had to be downstairs with breakfast no later than seven-thirty. I fixed breakfast and started dinner and I unloaded the kitchen table and loaded up the dishwasher. Then I would go into the children's bedroom and start my day's work. I had to do laundry twice a week and iron twice a week. Every wash day you'd wash in the mornin and in the afternoon you would iron all evenin plus you would fix dinner, serve dinner, and then wash the dishes. In the meantime, while doin all this, you'd be answerin telephones, answerin doorbells. You'll be right in the middle of doin a whole lot of work, and you got the houselady, the owner of the house—she's sittin there readin the paper, she's sittin back with a cigarette, and now she's right there by the door, she could get up and open the door—and she would call you, "Laetitia, come and answer the door please." And I am right in the middle of a whole lot of workin; the sweat is just fallin, and I got to stop what I'm doin, I got to go answer the door. The telephone rings. Now she's right by the phone. Instead of pickin up the phone, answerin the phone, she would call me, "Laetitia, answer the phone and if it is somebody for me tell them I'll be right there." Now she is sittin right by the phone, but she's readin the paper so hard or readin some book tellin how she can keep beautiful and everything. And you got to stop all this. This makes you behind schedule, and you got to try to get yourself back to the time so you can be ready to go to the next thing you got to do, so you could be able to get off work in the time you supposed to be gettin off. By the time I got off work I would be so tired I didn't feel like takin a shower or a bath. I'd be so tired, when I'd get up next mornin, I'd still be tired.

Sometimes it comes to a point that they see that you do this and you don't say anything—then they add on two or three more things the next day for you to do. This comes to be habit-forming, and you find yourself just getting tired and nervous and everything. And then they say to you like this—"I know it's a lot of work, but this has to be done. I know you're not a machine." But at the same time, they usin you as if you are a machine—like you got three or four hands. Now some of these things that they ask you to do is really nothin that they couldn't just get up and just do it and let you go on to the basic things that you know that are there to do. But see, them womens, they get so lazy and they feel like, "I got a maid. Why not let her do it?" That is the attitude they bring out. I mean, this is what they really show you. You can tell, you can tell—they don't have to say, "Well, Laetitia, you are my maid. You do so-and-so, and so you do this, and you do that." They sugarcoat you in a way. You are very much sugarcoated. Like, "Oh, you're such a nice person. You're beautiful. But will you please do so-and-so." And, "Laetitia, if you don't mind, will you please step inside and bring me so-and-so." With these little simple things that they could just get right up on their feet and just walk into the room and get it and come back, and I could go on my basic ways. But the more you do for them people, the more they want for you to do. As far as I am concerned, your work with them is never ended. And if there comes a time that you refuse to do something, this is when you can really see that what you have been doin has been in vain. What I mean is that you are not really satisfyin these peoples as far as the work is concerned because they don't think you get tired. And when you come to the point that you just can't go on with this no longer, that you are about to explode, you gotta just stop and catch yourself to keep from tellin these people what you really think.

The last job that I was on I did come to the point that I told this lady, "What do you think, I'm a machine or somethin?"

She said, "No, no, no, I don't think you are a machine, but there is work in this house, Laetitia, and lots of work."

I said, "Well, I tell you something—put yourself in the place of me; just forget about who you are and put yourself in the position that you are putting me in. Do you think that you could turn out the work that I turn out in a day? I come to your job ten o'clock in the mornin and I leave sometimes ten-thirty at night. My sons can tell you the times I have walked into the house when I will be so tired that I fall over on my bed, and I have to rest awhile before I get up and do anything." And I work on her job, and she had the nerve to tell me that "I don't think you're doing too much work." And I'm about to drop, just feel like droppin dead. If I was really to sit down then, I wouldn't even get up. That's how exhausted I would be.

I never had a job just workin for a man, but they say it is much better to just work for a man than to work for a woman. A woman, she's bossy. And they are more prejudiced. And, you know somethin, you go into their home and they'll watch you. If they have a husband they'll watch you, and like if they tell you to go and make up the bedroom and they find out that their husband is still in the bedroom or bathroom, they will say, "Oh, let me check to see if Mr. So-and-So is in there." And they will run back, "Oooh, don't go in there now. Wait for my husband to finish. He will be out in just one moment." You know right there, they don't trust you—not when it comes down to around their men. But yet and still, they can trust you to cook for them. That is the part I could never understand. You only there for one thing, that is to work and to get your money and leave there. What I care about your man? I ain't thinkin about your man. And the part that I never could understand—now they don't trust you doin around their husband and certain things, but they'll trust to eat your food. And that is the most important or dangerous part right there. I'm cookin your food. If I was that type of person and I really got a mean streak in me, I could poison you to death. But all these things they look over. They only care about simple things like gettin all the work they can out of you. That is the things they look forward to. And they don't seem to care nothin about your sympathy, or "I know you got to work, but you got responsibility at home and your obligations there." They don't seem to care about what you got to do at your house or where you got children or family back at your house. All they care about is what you could do for them. They pay you a little bit of money, and they think you supposed to be satisfied and not say nothin about a raise or nothin. "I can't pay no more money. I mean, look how much I'm payin you." They are not payin you nothin! Really nothin.

All the peole I have worked for, basically all these jobs were the same way, same problems—they don't hardly have time to ask you about your background or how it was when you was comin up. See, that is the part—they don't seem to be concerned about nothin about you—how you come up, or how it was with you, or anything about in your home, or how you get along, or how you can do this, and how you can live off this little bit of money—they don't even approach you with things like that. All them peoples know to approach you with is how to do this in my house, and you must do this, and you must do that. And the time that you say no to somethin, they get mad at you. That is all they know. They took no interest in me or my family. They don't even ask you—they might ask you how many children you got, and that is it. If it comes down to the part of askin you who takes care of the children while you workin here for them, they don't even ask. Nothin!

Sometimes, if they was watchin somethin on TV, they might ask me, "Laetitia, what do you think about so and so? What do you think about the civil rights movement? What's goin on down South? Do you think that it is right that they should do so-and-so?"

I would say, "Well, I think that so-and-so should be doin this."

They say, "Well, what can you do? What can you say?" They gonna cut that conversation very short because they don't really want to know what you feel. It'll bug you. It builds up thoughts in your mind. It really sometimes makes you come to the point—you want to explode. You want to just come out and ask them, "Why you don't never ask me about my family? Why you don't never ask me questions about what happens to me or how I grew up or somethin? Why don't you really talk about the black race, or how I feel about certain things that's goin on with the civil rights movement?" All this you want to talk about, but you never get the opportunity cause they always cut the conversation short. Very short. And they go back to something that is beneficial for them. They are interested in one thing—that I do my work. It is like they're tellin me, "If you hold a conversation with me, then you ain't gonna be gettin too much of the work that I want done. It is gonna slow you up. So, other than to have a conversation with you about your work, we are not even gonna talk, so you can go gettin back to my domestic work." That is the whole point right there. It makes you very angry. You can see this thing happenin right there before your eyes. The way that you are bein treated and the way you have to hurry up for this and that. Did you see this picture, "The Odd Couple," that comes on TV? Check it out. You see how the mother is runnin—that is it. They don't want to hear nothin, believe me—"Just do your work, cause we ain't got time to be talking about nothin, cause if you talk about somethin you are not going to get my work done."

If there is such a place as they call heaven, them people is in heaven now. I know that. The luxury that they live in—you just look at these beautiful things. What comfort is it serving, really? It's something on the wall or something on the shelf, and you got to be so particular with it. They call these things antiques, you know. What is the word my mother's mother used to use? They used to call it in the South their "treasures." And it is a treasure—"I don't want anything to happen to it, so be careful with this. I wouldn't have it get broken for nothin." But yet and still somethin can happen to *me*. They'll put me up on a great big ladder up there to wash the windows, if I ain't got no more sense than to get up. They ain't worried about me fallin off that ladder. Do you see what I'm talkin about? That's the things you can see, little things like that. Somethin they got just sittin there on the shelf, somethin on the wall—oooh, you got to hold it so careful, you got to be so particular, you got to make sure nothin happens to it. *Me* they don't care about. They put me in a position that anything can happen to me. They care less. All they care is to work you to death and pay you just the less salary they can pay you. All they worry about is what they got in that house—and their money, how to save their money, to pay you a little salary, and how to keep the rest of the money so they can live happily ever after. And you just doin all the work while they sit back in luxury—you workin yourself almost down to the ground, and they payin you a litle bit of money. And they don't want you to say nothin.

There are some things that get to me and make me feel bad. You don't feel so good about uniforms. It is not a good feelin because it makes you feel, well, like I'm not as good as they are, because look at me, I'm doin their dirty work. Sometimes they want you to clean their white floors and things. A lot of them have these white marble floors and they want you to get on your knees and clean. It begins to grow in your mind that I'm not as good as they are, because, look at me, I have to do this kind of work to make a dollar, and they sittin up lookin at you and standin over you tellin you every five minutes—do this and do that. It really gives you a different feelin, I cannot say that it don't.

They spend a lot of money on clothin. That is another thing. Like, you watch them when they get dressed, and they come out, and most of the time—oh, they like a lot of attention, you know. They like for you to tell them, "Oh, you look nice; you look pretty today! Oh, I wish I could go out and be rich and look like you! Oh, that is so nice!" Now, they like that. You should see. They like you to talk about how they look. They don't see that sometimes you walk in and look nice when you get there. They see you walk in, but they wouldn't even think enough of you to say, "You look nice this mornin." That's the picture that I get—that they don't really have time to look at you, because once you get inside the door you goin straight to your room to change into your uniform. They really never see you no more than work.

These people are not happy, uh-uh, because they are at the point—their life is like on a string, a string that stretches from day to day. They got most of everything, but it's just somethin lacking. They got everything, but they still not happy because they are worried so about keepin what they got. They can't be happy because they worry too much about gettin everything else they can get and keepin what they got too. And not havin to let any of it go for nothin. They're not happy and they have nothin to do. Let's face it—you sittin down every day with nothin to do, and you got a maid, somebody walkin all around you every day, that you can tell, "Do this and do that." You can't be happy like that. No, that is not a happy life. But you know they don't know what's a happy life—they never experienced enough to see if it is a happy life. They don't know nothin about it, because from childhood on up they always had somebody to take care of them and do their work. They have no satisfaction. That's the whole point. They have nothin to do; they're restless. You got to get a certain amount of energy off, right. So it comes to nothin but bug your maid and say, "Do this and do that" all day, and think of a thousand things to do in one hour's time. Most of these womens is like that. They don't even work. All they do is stay home all day. Maybe they run out for a couple of hours—go shoppin, go buy clothes, or buy somethin for the house. That is all they have to do. They spend their day spendin money, or just sit home. And that's nothin.

Listen, they go out and spend double the money in one day that they gonna pay you for the whole week. They go out and pay fifty, sixty, seventy dollars for one pair of shoes, four, five hundred dollars for one dress, a gown. Now they probably won't put that gown on but maybe two times, cause they buyed it for a certain occasion—"I need a gown, and I must go out and get this gown. And I'm having to wear this tonight over to such-and-such. There is a party goin on." And they go out and spend all that money, and then when you ask for a raise, they can show you all kind of points and bring out all kind of things why they can't give you a raise right now. But yet and still, they're spendin money every day. And what they're buyin, they don't really need. It's just, "I have the money, I can afford to buy it, so I did." That's the kind of life they live. Now that's not a happy life. Believe me, it's not happy. Oh, they will try to impress you that they are happy. Look, you get into one room and let them be in another—like the man and woman is sittin there and they're discussin somethin. Most of the time that man is givin the woman the business about how she went out and did this today and she went out and did that today. They have problems, like everybody else, but they can afford to give you the brush-off because they got plenty of money.

I can be not happy, I can be not satisfied, but unless I can see where it's gonna mean somethin to discuss the matter with you, then I keep it to myself. I restrain myself with tryin to talk with them people. There's no need to discuss your matters with them. I'm a black person—they're not even interested in knowin you. I just got to live, that's all.

I can tell the difference in my health, cause like five years ago I could do a little bit more—like more faster, more swifter. I've slowed down quite a bit, and that comes from that rushin. It really takes a lot out of you. We should be gettin not under three-fifty to four dollars an hour, a hundred and fifty dollars a week. Domestic work is hard work. It's not easy at all. It's hard.

Arletta Michaels

ARLETTA MICHAELS IS AN ENERGETIC, SPIRITED WOMAN—NOT EVEN THE MOST attentive transcription can suggest the lively movement of her Jamaican dialect. I spoke with her twice, once in each employer's apartment, and she seemed completely at home in both places. During the first interview, little Jonathan hovered in Arletta's vicinity and interrupted us occasionally—just to make it clear that he did not really approve of my diverting her attention away from him. After our second interview, I leaned over and kissed Arletta lightly on the cheek as I was leaving. We'd both enjoyed our talk; we'd laughed together and been comfortable with one another—and when it came to saying goodbye, it felt distant, too "professional" merely to shake hands, so I kissed her and stepped out into the hallway to wait for the elevator. And as we stood there Arletta began to rub her hand over the spot where I'd planted my kiss.

*M*y name is Arletta Michaels, and I was born 1941, the twenty-eighth of September, in Spanish Town, it's a little town near Kingston. We grew up on a sugar farm, very large—The United Fruit Company, they grow sugar cane, bananas, and things like that. My father works as a supervisor on the farm—gives out the work to the farmers, makes up the payroll. My grandparents were from India. I think they from Calcutta. I didn't know my grandfather, but I knew my grandmother and she sit down and tell us that she came here on a boat, and the government put them in a barracks and let them work like for a penny a day. You know, long time ago. And then things started to get civilized—new governments and things like that.

My mother and father was born in Jamaica, grew up in Jamaica. My mother got married to my father when she was fourteen years old and my father was seventeen. She had ten of us, but two died in childbirth and one died of typhoid fever. We were poor in one way, but we weren't poor on food, and we had a nice house to live in—it was very neat, very clean, very nice. We have four rooms—the boys, they share one room; the girls shares one room; my mother and father share one room—then we have a little living room, a veranda, and a kitchen and a toilet to the back.

Growin up, we get up like four o'clock in the morning. Then we go to a little sink in the backyard, a pipe with running water, and we wash our face, brush our teeth. We didn't have toothbrush at those times—we used chew sticks. So we get up at four o'clock. My brothers go with my father to get the cow milked, and we girls go in the kitchen, help our mother cook breakfast. By six o'clock my mother and father left the house, and we get ready and walk to Catholic elementary school. We walk to school barefooted, about a mile and a half. We loved it as kids cause we were mixed up together at school—Indians, Negroes, Chinese, and some English whites. It wasn't like here—how do you say?—like prejudice here. It was a lotta different kids. And after school my friends come to my home—and no matter who, we all combine. My mother put on one big iron pot with dumpling, banana, West Indian food—and when she put the food on the table, everybody eats. Nobody say their skin white, their skin black—we all eat from one another, we share.

So we did that then. Now, my father get a promotion and we buy a piece of land so he can start to build a house. It took us five years and we worked very hard helping carry the sand to make the house. I was fourteen now, and in Jamaica they look husband for you when you were young. Your parents let people know you're growin up and come from a decent background. When I say decent—we are poor, but we do not go raggedy, you know—we have one suit of clothes that's clean, and our parents working. So my parents come to your parents and say, "Well, my daughter is growing up. How about they engage, and when they get bigger they married?" So the parents would go out and get the husband for the daughter, and the daughter doesn't know anything. When you reach like fifteen, they have a get-together and you meet your husband. Well, that didn't happen to me, cause when I was fourteen I got pregnant. See, our parents, they doesn't sit down and teach us anything about sex life. They hide everything from us. My mother tell me baby come in plane.

After I had my child, I left my parents and dropped out of school. I said, "I take up my own responsibility," and I left my child with my mother and went to Kingston to work. I got job in restaurants, but I still could come back and visit my mother and buy things for my child. And I worked and I worked my way—I work in factories, I work in restaurants, I work in hotels. The only work I didn't do in Jamaica was domestic work because that doesn't pay anything there. I'm not going to say I was pretty or anything, but I was nice—and I had a lotta boyfriends in Kingston. The boys in Jamaica don't care, you know—like here, you has to be a high society people to get a boyfriend. In Jamaica it's different—you go into the street, a guy says, "Hi, how are you?" and you get friendly, he takes you out to dinner. Then maybe something happen to you and you become friendship, and then you go for a period of time till something maybe happen again. Those days I got Chinese boyfriend; I got white boyfriend—English boy; I got black boyfriend. I never had no Indian boyfriend because I never like Indian like myself. It was nice, and I have a lotta fun. Work here, work there, and struggle my way to come to New York; I went out and I struggle my way.

Well, New York now. I work in a hotel, and I met this very nice white lady, American—one of those, I say, high society. She asked me if I wanted to come to New York, and I tell her yes. It wasn't hard, like now, to come here. All you need is a letter of invitation. So she send me a letter and I got a visa and came up in 1968. As I said before, I was happy in Jamaica, and I had a lotta boyfriends, but I did want to travel and try to get something in my head and realize what things was all about. I met people in the hotel, and they telling me, "Oh, you should go to New York! New York is this, and New York is that." So that get me excited, wanna come to New York.

Well, I come—just bring few piece of clothes. I bring a pair of white shoes, because, you know, in Jamaica girls dress in white shoes. So I buy a pair white shoes for fifteen dollars, and that's what I wear to New York, with a nice little dress. I come to Kennedy Airport—it was like I was in a different world. I was freezing in my little dress, it was cold, so the stewardess wrap me up in a blanket. And then I was nervous; I was trembling but I didn't cry or anything like that. But I'm saying to myself, "I'm coming to a strange country, I haven't no relatives here." You know, different crazy ideas. And after I get to her apartment, it looked like prison to me. I couldn't get used to peeping through the hole in the front door; I couldn't get adjusted to the food. And sleeping at night—I couldn't sleep cause I wasn't relaxed. I wasn't accustomed to being with white people. In Jamaica I visit whites, but not to live with. Here I was living with this family. They were different in a way—I can't describe it to you, but they were different. You know, like I have to drink out of different cup; I have a special plate to eat on. I was like outer space, like I have a disease and they don't want to catch it.

I miss everybody. I miss my whole family. I was homesick because that was my first time traveling, and didn't have no relatives in America. People telling you, "Go to America!" I didn't realize I was going to see rats; I didn't realize I was going to see man walking dirty and stink on the street; I didn't realize I was going to see garbage pile up; I didn't realize

I was going to see slum area. I mean, you got slum area in Jamaica, but you know that because you come from there and you see. But going to a different country and people telling you, "Oh, you should take a trip to New York"—when you come to New York, it's a different thing. I see rat on Broadway—biggest I see in my whole life. And really, I was homesick, homesick and neglected. But I'm like this—I don't say anything to anybody. I sit down and cry to myself, said my Hail Mary, and I pray and said, "One day things will come my way." Many times I feel like I'm not wanted. Then I think twice and said, "Well, I've come here to better my position." So I make up my mind, and after awhile I got used to it, and it didn't bother me anymore.

Finally, I work and make friends, other Jamaican girls you meet in the park minding the kids. They be here longer than I and they tell me the routines—give me a lowdown, what's goin on. We bring the kids to the park—then the kids would go play, and someone would say, "Are you from Jamaica?"

I say, "Yes."

And she would say, "Where you working?"

I say, "Working next door. I just came here couple of weeks ago."

"Well, I've been here from like 1955." You know, just speaking. Then she says, "How much a week you make?"

"Forty dollars."

"What you do for forty dollars?"

"Well, I've got to cook, wash, iron, clean the house, and take care of the kids."

She says, "Oh child, you stupid! Quit that job! Work on for a couple of weeks while I find you another job."

So I quit and got a job for this woman in Queens. Oh my God, she was a pain in the neck! You work and they leave you a list from here to Broadway. I mean, everybody like their house clean, and everybody like special things done—but you be there for a certain period of months, and they be leaving you the same list. You be doing it over and over again. And when Friday come for her to pay me, seems like it's so hard for her to give you your money. "Oh, Arletta, I forgot to go to the bank. Can you wait till Monday?" That's no way to take care of business. I come and clean her house—I'm her maid, let's put it that way—I do what she have to do. When Friday come, pay me and let me go. Don't tell me, "Wait till Monday!" I got bills to take care of, too. What they think I live off of? Fresh air?

Well, I met my husband, got married, and everything, and I become hip to everything what's going on. He's American—black. His parents are from Jamaica. They came here in 1908 and he was born on the Lower East Side in 1930 something—I've forgotten, but he's forty-six years old, so figure it out. He move with the blacks and the whites, because he works in the Bronx Terminal Market, and they mixed there. When someone messes with him, he curse them out—and that's about it. Well, my job was getting on my nerves, aggravating me—and I'm a type of person, if something happens, I'm afraid to tell you in front of your face. I'm not that bulky type of person—I'll go home and cry and I'll sit and tell my husband. So he tell me, "Don't do this, Arletta! Don't let those white people push you around, because I've been through this. I know what some of them think, because I was a kid in the street, selling newspapers and selling ice. Don't be afraid to talk to them cause there's only one thing they can tell you—'Quit!' And you can get another job." But I used to be afraid when I first came here. You know, when you first come into a country, you get panicky.

Then I started work in a factory, and I have a supervisor, and you have to push time—and when I get my little money, they take out tax and I don't come home with nothing. So I said, "To heck with everything—if I find a good family I can work with, I work for them and that's it." Then I come to Laura.

I like Laura, and I like Tom—they're very nice. They don't tell me, "Do this!" They don't push me around or anything like that. I been working for her now, going four years. I don't mind this kind of work, you know. I like to do it. But I like to work for people who understand and treat me like a human being. Like Laura—Laura is a wonderful person—I work for her from now until the day I die. And Karen, across the way, I feel the same for her, too. For as long as I been in this country—I swear to God, cross my heart—those are the two person I work for that being a maid doesn't make no difference. I say this—you can put this in the book—I'm poor, and money means a lot to me, but appreciation is better than money. Let me tell you—*appreciation*. If I have a cup of coffee with Laura, she would take that cup and sip from it. The kids would eat from my plate. Her kids come to my house and stay the night. And she's been to my house—she see where I live, so she have respect for me. She loves me—she don't like me, she loves me. And she treats me just like she treats another *white* person—let's put it that way. She treats me like she treats another white person, and she's not prejudiced.

Karen and her family is in this building too. She's the only black woman I've worked for, and she's married to a white man. She treats me beautiful. Some people, you work for them, but you can't sit and eat and talk to them like how I would with Laura and Karen. I come in the morning, Karen'll be here drying the dishes. She'll say, "Arletta, would you care for a cup of coffee?"

I say, "All right," and she make the coffee. I say, "You don't have to do it."

She say, "Oh, come on girl, sit down."

"Karen, you better go in the bedroom and let me go do my work."

"Come on, girl, sit down and talk."

You see, she makes me feel *welcome*—she don't make me feel I'm just a maid cleaning her house. She treat me equal, just like a friend—and I think that's a good relationship between a maid and employer. We talk about sex life, and things like that. One time she ask me about my son. I said, "My son is a mixture—his father is half-Chinese, his grandmother on his father's side is black woman, and I'm Indian. In Jamaica we say he's mixed blood."

So she said if she and her husband have a child, they would consider it as a black child. I said, "No, I consider that child to be a mixed-blood child like mine."

She said, "No Arletta, if Arthur and I have a child now, they would consider it black in America."

I love Laura's boy Jonathan like my own child, and I handle him like I would handle my child. He got a temper, a high temper, and sometimes when he do something and I punish him, he goes to Laura and tell her a different thing. But Laura cooperate with me—she listen to my idea most of the time. Like one time Jonathan helped me set the dining table. He's telling me, "This chair is for Laura, this is for Tom, this is for Bill, and this is for me."

I said to him, "So I can't sit at the table! Let me tell you something—I got a dining table in my house, and I got four chairs too, and I can sit anywhere I want to sit. You have been to my house, and I didn't tell you, 'This chair is for my husband, this chair is for me, and this chair is for my friend.' You sit anywhere you want to sit, and you eat anything you want to eat."

"I don't care," he said.

I said, "Well, I care! I care because I'm the one who's working here, and I keep this house clean. So you don't tell me this here chair is for Laura, this chair is for Tom, and that chair for Billy. Where you want me to sit and eat? On the floor?"

"You can't sit at the table!" he said.

"Oh yeah? That's what you telling me? Okay, you don't want me to sit at the table, I don't have to sit at the table. And let me tell you something—any time you are here by yourself, I will fix your lunch and you sit at the table by yourself. I'll never sit here with you again if I don't sit at this table tonight with you all!"

When the family came in for dinner, I took the stool and sit in the kitchen. Laura came up and said, "Arletta, what's the matter?"

I said, "Jonathan don't want me to sit at the table and eat."

So she said, "Come on, Arletta, sit at the table."

I said, "No, Laura, I'm not coming because Jonathan insists for me not sitting at the table, and I'm not coming to sit there. I'm waiting until when Jonathan don't have no friends over, and when you is not home—let him sit by himself and see how it feels to eat by himself."

And she talked to him, "Jonathan, why you say that to Arletta? You know you hurt her feelings."

He said he's sorry, and it's finished right there—but I put him in his place, and he learned. You are there working, and the parents is not there—you have to learn them how to treat you. I believe in having manners. This word may sound funny to you, but in Jamaica we grow up with manners. My parents teach me with principle and respect. If you do something wrong, you get your behind beat by a strap. That's punishment! You learn to behave, and you get principle.

I teach Jonathan a little principle. Yesterday, for instance, he has this little friend come to the park with him. I sent Jonathan to buy me an ice cream, so he get it and hand it to his friend—"Here, Stevie Hall, give it to Arletta."

His friend just throw it on the bench, like feeding a dog. I said, "Let me tell you something, I'm not a god-damn dog—I'm a human being like you! When I give you your lunch today, I didn't throw it on the table like that, treat you like a god-damn dog. Don't you do it! I don't like it, and I don't want the ice cream. You can have it."

I don't like things like that. A child have to learn to treat the person who is taking care of them like a human being. So I teach him principle. When he comes here to visit Jonathan, he will have it in his mind—nobody treat her like a maid. Little things like that hurts my feelings.

One time I asked the boys, "Would you like to come to my house?"
They said, "Sure!"
So I said, "Laura, is it all right for Jonathan and Billy to come?"
She said, "Sure, why not?"

I said, "But don't call me up on the telephone five, six times, because nothing is wrong with them and nothing will happen. You're allowed one call, and that's it."

Then I tell the children, "My neighborhood isn't all white kids, and my building isn't fabulous like this. We're going to see a lot of black kids because we're going to visit my friends, and they're black."

They didn't care. My friend Judy, she got three kids, and the boys went off with them. They played games together, they drank soda—it was no difference to them. They were running around the house and everything. They visit me a few times after that, and they love it. And they eats anything I cook—barbecue spare ribs, black-eye peas on rice, fricassee chicken. They don't tell me they don't want it—they love it. And Laura only called once.

When she went away to California the first time, I stayed with those kids. I said, "Only two calls, no more. Those kids are under my responsibility, and I wouldn't do nothing to hurt anybody's kids." You see, I'd been working there a long time then. I said, "Don't call every two minutes to find out—the kids will get very panicky and nervous; they won't feel safe with me, they won't feel relaxed." Billy was seven then, and when Laura and Tom went away, he slept in the bed with me. We talk and talk each night—we talk about school, we talk about all different things. He tells me history, little things that I don't really have knowledge to know about, things he learn in school. We talk about baseball stars and movie stars.

He says to me, "Arletta, is there a lot of black stars?"

I said, "Sure, they got a lot of black stars. If you go to the movies, you see them. And they have high society black people. But, you know, in every group you have good people and bad—that's what's important. Don't think *black* people, *white* people." You see, I make them think. They have to respect me—I'm a human being. And they are learning.

So I'm happy working for Laura and Karen. I can sit and eat with the family, but if there's company I don't feel like sit at the table with them—I'm going to the maid's room and have my coffee by myself. Let them discuss what they have to discuss. One time Laura said, "Arletta, I'm having a friend over for lunch. We'll have it in the kitchen with you."

I said, "Oh no, you and your friend go in the dining room." See, if there's she and me alone, I feel more relaxed. But if she have a friend that I don't know, I get uptight. They might say, "Well how come you has your maid sitting at the table eating with you?" People do that—they think I'm going in their category. Let me do my work here and go home.

I got a nice apartment now, and my husband and I, we live very comfortable. He makes a good salary and he hits his number a couple of times, so he drive a Cadillac. He like Cadillacs. When he pay for this one, he trades again. He don't get 1977, but he loves Cadillac, and what he loves, he buys. You see, I classify myself here as a maid, but when I finish and go through that door, I'm no more maid. I take off this raggedy dress, change my clothes, step downstairs—I'm finished, I'm a human being. I have a nice home and husband—people show me respect.

I feel this way now—as soon as I work another five years, I'm getting out of this country. I just want to buy me a nice little house in Jamaica, rent out part, work six months in New York, and save me seven or eight hundred dollar. I've been through this, and I'm only giving myself another five years—then I say goodbye. And now my son is growin up and will be graduating from the Police Academy in Jamaica. Then he will travel and improve himself. Someday he may be an inspector of police. So I got a son who is bringing me up in the world, that people can have respect for me—and I'm very proud of that. I don't want you getting me wrong—I'm not ashamed of doing this kind of work. I love doin it—and the two people I'm working for now, I work for them till the day come that I can't do it anymore. But I'm not waiting for that day to come.

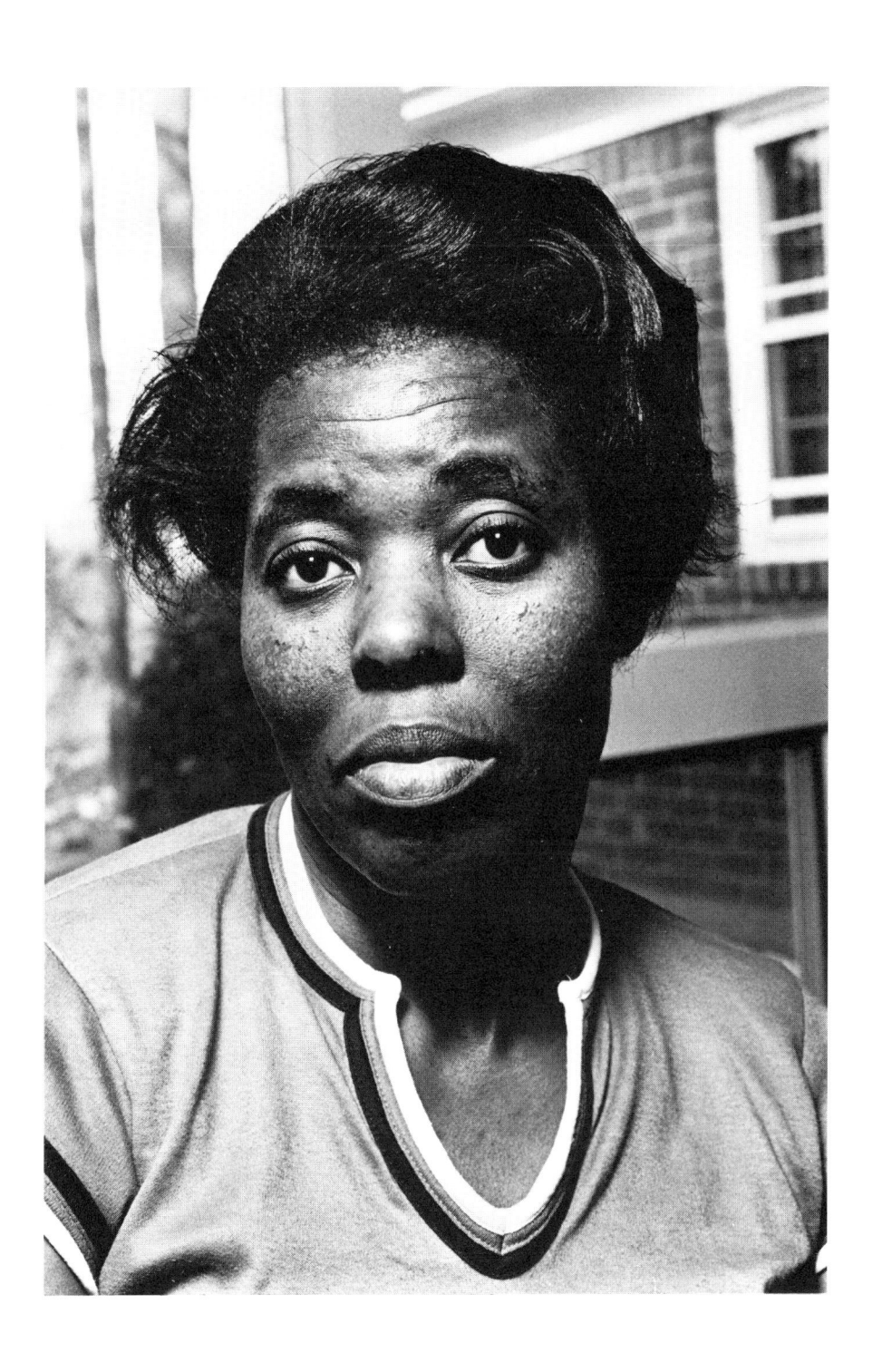

Minnie Stevens

AT ONE POINT IN OUR INTERVIEW MINNIE STEVENS RECALLED HOW SHE HAD spoken to Lynn just before my arrival. "I don't know how much Bob's gonna get from me," she told Lynn, "because I haven't had many terrible experiences. You know, I haven't had anything that was really dramatic." When I called Minnie to set up our interview, I never told her I was looking for unpleasant experiences, and yet I accept her remarks as an instructive parody, not only of my work, but of many writers engaged in similar projects. When you conceive of a book intended to explore some complex social issue, it implies that a problem exists—Minnie understood that, typically, it is "terrible experiences" that make up the "really dramatic" material that our media feeds its audience. But what Minnie showed me, both in her narrative and in her everyday relations with the Ross family, is that in America few things are more dramatic or moving than those occasions in which blacks and whites are able to show interest and affection for one another unselfconsciously and unafraid.

*M*y name is Minnie Stevens. I'm thirty-nine years old, and I was born in Cheraw, South Carolina—it's small, very small. A great-aunt raised me; she said she and my uncle took me at nine months old. So these are the parents I can remember.

We lived on a farm, sharecroppin, and I hated farm work, but I worked—I really worked. I couldn't stand pickin cotton. I hated it. I didn't mind pullin fodder or choppin cotton, but I hated to pick—and I always used to say, "If I ever get grown, I will never pick cotton again." And I want you to know, I haven't picked any since either.

I guess I had a normal life for a southerner. I hear people say they used to be hungry, and I can't say that. It might not've been what I wanted, but I've always had food. As I said, my uncle was a good farmer, and he provided. We sharecropped for a white man, Mr. Sam Jones. I thought they were very nice people. As a matter of fact, his wife always sent me Christmas cards. And every time I go home, I go to see them, because I grew up with these people. Maybe we're gettin a little ahead now, but I feel that some of those people down there was much better than some of the people here. You know, there are people that have experiences here that they didn't have in the South—you know, with some of those people they work for. I read those parts of the book you sent me—I can't believe they happened, even though I heard the people talk.

And there were white kids, Campbells I think they was, that had a daughter. She musta been my age, and we used to play together. I don't know—I guess it was a normal life. And I can't remember any black people that had any terrible experience around me. I guess I probably felt about those white peoples like I did anybody—they was nice to me, and I liked em. I'm sure we musta had thoughts, but maybe it wasn't anything that really bothered us. And my aunt used to work for white people, and I used to baby-sit for the kids. I don't know, we all seemed to love each other. I always say, "There are some dirty ones, and there some good ones." Maybe we were just lucky. You know somethin, I didn't hear about the Klan until I considered myself grown. I didn't know those kinda peoples existed; I never heard of anybody bein lynched around me.

Always in high school I was gonna be a nurse. Maybe I just liked the idea of takin care of people or somethin—I was always gonna be a nurse. I liked the white uniform, maybe that was it. I had this friend—we went to school from first grade right up until we finished high school together—and we were gonna go to college together. We started off at Clinton College. I went for about four weeks, and I couldn't stand it. I was homesick; I cried the whole time. She kept goin, but I quit. I went home and stayed around there for awhile, and I decided to come to New York. I don't even know how that came about. I think about that sometime—I say, "How could I? I was so homesick at college." But I came to New York, and I've been here twenty years.

I think it was a friend of mine who I hadn't seen for years—she found in a newspaper where people wanted women to sleep in, and she approached me with it and said, "Let's go!" I said, "Okay," and we sent away in. They sent us tickets and everything, and we made our plans and packed up. My aunt, bein who she is, you know—"All right, you don't like it, here's your money for your fare back home." She had been to New York at one point, and she kept sayin, "You won't like it; you won't like the way the people cook their food," and that kinda thing.

We came by Trailways bus, and we spent a night in Norfolk. They gave us breakfast the next mornin—scrambled eggs and somethin—and then we got back on the bus and came to New York. I can't remember much. I was inside the bus terminal wonderin what's gonna happen next. Somebody from the agency met us and put us on the Long Island Railroad. This agency was right near the Freeport Station; we must've gotten there about nine in the mornin. There was a bunch of us—people from other places I didn't know. And by nine-thirty I was gone. This man come in and he talked to me—he decided he liked me; he talked to the lady, and he took me home. This was my first job, just from home, they knew that I didn't have any experience or anything—but I guess there musta been somethin about me he liked. I said somethin about my girlfriend, and the lady said, "Well, give her your number, and when she gets set she'll call you. You'll get in touch." And then he took me home. Maybe I was too young to be worried—is that possible? Cause as I think back, I couldn't have been too scared by it. I don't get scared too easy—I have a lotta nerve. I just get homesick.

It was only a man and wife and dog. At that time when you came through an agency, you got one hundred and twenty-five dollars a month, and they paid you every two weeks. My job was really nothin. The lady was in bed at that time—she had bone cancer; she couldn't move. I was just really a companion to her. My room was small but comfortable. All of em have small rooms—I've never figured that out. And I had a uniform. This was all new, but I guess it kinda fitted in. I was tellin Lynn, "I think they thought I was their child." You know, because I was small, that's the way she would treat me. Like she'd call and make my appointment for the beauty parlor, and saw to it that somebody got me there. So this was it. I'd sit and watch television with her. And I used to get in the window and wonder which way home was, and get kinda homesick and that kinda thing. I was determined I was gonna stay though.

She had friends who had sleep-in help that she knew, and she'd call them up. This one girl was very nice; her name was Sarah. She used to come and pick me up, and we'd go shoppin together and that kind of thing. Now, I don't buy anything, but then I had to buy something new every time. I was off Thursdays and every other Sunday, and I guess I spent my money as fast as I got it. But one thing—I would always send my mother enough. Then what was left, I'd spend. So Sarah and I would go shoppin or go to a movie, and then at night we used to go to a place called the Celebrity Club. Most of the people I met at the Celebrity Club were houseworkers—sleepin in or doin day work, or somethin like that. And the club used to have live stars, you know, big time. And I used to enjoy that. Somebody said it turned out to be a killin place, but at that time it was really nice.

I also met a boyfriend at that time. Don't ask me his name—I really don't remember. He was nice, but I don't know—maybe it was just the way I was brought up, maybe I didn't care so much, because even at home I remember boys used to annoy me. Not because I didn't like em—maybe it was because I had this one fellow at home who everybody said loved me to death—and he used to always insist on comin to see me. It would really drive me up a wall. I hated it. And my aunt thought he was the nicest person goin. She used to say, "If you can't be nice to him, then isn't anybody else comin here."

And I used to say, "I don't care!" I really meant it—that's the way I was.

Then my uncle would see him comin or somethin, and he'd say, "Here come the preacher!" That would make my aunt angry because she said he was encouragin me to be mean to this fellow. But I really couldn't—to this day I can't stand the guy.

So Thursday nights I went to the Celebrity Club, but my Sundays off was a little worse because there was no black churches around. That bothered me because I was used to goin to church on Sunday—that was my one big thing. So for a long time, my Sundays was spent in the house.

Finally, the woman died. She got sick and they had to take her into the hospital. After about six weeks, her friend said to me, "I don't think she's comin back home, Minnie." I was sad; I was upset cause I really liked her. Then I started work for her friend.

At this time I had started to get around more. I don't know where I lost touch with Sarah—I think she went back home. But I had met other girls, and I'd go with them to the Community Bar or Franklin Bar and Grill. And the thing is, I don't drink. Most of the places had live entertainment, so it was nice just to sit and listen to the music, or somethin like that. One thing that made me kinda cautious—you meet a man and they say they're not married, and the next thing you know, they are married. This first guy I met, he's gone by the wayside—I don't know what he did. But then I met a young man who was in the service. He was very nice. On Thursdays he used to come and pick me up, and we'd go out together. The three girls in the family I worked for loved him to death. He'd call and I couldn't get the phone from them. Once the mother said, "Minnie, I don't know whether he's pickin up you or the girls," because they really—wow!

I worked for them until I decided I was goin back to South Carolina. I went home to stay—I wasn't comin back. I stayed for a couple of years, doin housework for the same people my family sharecropped. I certainly wasn't pickin cotton, believe me—I wouldn't do that again. I probably woulda stayed, but I had a cousin who was in New York, workin in Roslyn, and when she came home she said she knew this lady that wanted somebody to work. My cousin said, "Why don't you come? You'll be near me." And I guess this made a difference—she started tellin me about her church. Sure enough, I came to Roslyn, and I worked for this family for a long time.

Back in Roslyn I started roomin with a girl named Lorraine. She and I became very good friends—and we're still good friends. There was a couple more girls with us. Henrietta—everybody thought we were sisters, cause you didn't see one without the other. We used to always go together. There's one girl from Alabama who's still livin there. Lorraine and I, we started to bowl. I don't know what even made us decide to go on the bowlin alley—neither one of us knew anything about it. Now, I'm all right, but then we weren't doin anything. We used to throw the balls in the gutter, and there was a gentleman, we called him Jay, he was a nice man, he said, "If you girls don't stop that, I'm gonna have to move the gutter in the center of the lane." He showed us how to keep score, he showed us about bowlin—he really started us. And now today I have a hundred sixty-three average—I know what I'm doin.

I was datin guys at that time—a guy who lived in the city and a guy who lived out in Brooklyn. It didn't make any difference. I don't think I fell in love with anybody. Then Lorraine and I decided we'd move on and get our own apartment. It's kinda hard for young girls to get apartments, cause a lotta people don't wanta be bothered—they say, "You'll have a lotta men; you're on welfare"—somethin like that. But they musta liked us, cause they accepted us. We knew they didn't want children, but we didn't have any kids at the time. So we lived there a long time—until I got pregnant. I musta been in love by then, right? We knew we had to get another apartment because they didn't want unmarried women with kids—and I wasn't gonna get married. We started lookin for an apartment again, and this time it was harder. I don't know whether it's kids that're so bad, or welfare. Most people hate to have welfare people, and I can understand it. There are some, they tear up peoples' houses. We really went through a lot before we finally got an apartment. Meantime, Lorraine got pregnant. Ha! She was pregnant already, as a matter of fact, cause her daughter's older than my daughter. Things were hard, but we were always workin. I worked the day my daughter was born.

My daughter's name is Leah. I had said, "If I have a girl I wanta name her somethin odd, somethin you don't hear every day." But I didn't know what.

So Lynn said, "Name her after me."

I said, "Lynn? You hear that all the time."

So she said, "No, my Hebrew name is Leah."

And this other lady I worked for says, "Minnie, I had a very good friend in college named Doreen, and I always thought that was a beautiful name."

So I named her Leah Doreen—and you don't hear it much either.

I'm still with Lynn and her family—nine years, goin into my tenth. I have my own apartment in town, and I'm here every day. They travel a lot, and I stay when they go away. Leah's in school here with Joshua and Sara. She comes up here every mornin to take the bus with them. They go to school, they play, they fight—they're together every day—and we go home at night.

I not only work for Lynn—I think she's my friend. We're really kinda close. We started off with a good relationship—it could be because she's a southerner—she's from Charleston, South Carolina. Everybody says we sound alike—so don't feel bad, you're not the only person that can't tell our voices on the phone. Everybody calls, even my friends, and they don't realize they're talkin to the wrong person. If there's somethin on my mind right now, I'd talk to Lynn. I'll talk to her, and she'll talk to me. My friends, everybody, they know we're very close.

Like Lynn can come in and tell me I'm prejudiced, you know—some things I'll say. And I admit it. One time I said to her, "There are some black peoples I wouldn't want to live next door to. I can understand why some white people don't wanta live next door to them, cause I don't either."

She said, "My God, you're more prejudiced than anybody else!"

I said, "No, it's just a fact, you know. I don't wanta be their neighbor, and this is it."

We can joke, you know—I'll say things to her I wouldn't dare say to some other people. Like one day Lynn and me was ridin along, and this lady was drivin like a jerk, even though she was a lady. So I said, "That Jewish lady!..."

Lynn said, "That lady's not Jewish."

So I says, "She's white and in New York—that makes her Jewish."

And Lynn cracked up. Our friendship just grew.

I see a lot of Larry. This is the first family that I ever worked for where I really saw a lot of the husband. I worked for a lady five years—I saw her husband once. But Larry is just like an old shoe. I've told Lynn, "You should be nice to him, he's a good man." It's unique. They send Leah to camp in the summer, right along with the kids. It's great—I have to admit it. "Uncle Larry," Leah calls him. She looks up to him, you know, she respects him. Uncle Larry can say somethin, and it's like God spoke; I can say it twenty times and nothin happens. He'll tell her, "I think you should read a book instead of watchin television"—and she doesn't give him any fuss. He said it, it's gospel. If I say the same thing, she'll say back, "I never watch television, I never get a chance." I'm happy that I got somebody who can help me along with her. I'll come in sometimes and say, "Uncle Larry, I think you need to have a talk with Leah." He'll say, "All right, Leah"—and this is it. I'm glad I have somebody I can turn to—it helps.

When they were in Califorina and I took care of the kids, they listened to me better than they do her. They know that if I say somethin, I mean it. I have a switch in there, and I use it—I don't play around. When it gets old and dry, I go out and get a new one from the dogwood tree. They get wild a lotta times, right. Sara, who is a lady, is very good—she never gives me any problems. But Joshua and Leah, they could make you climb a wall. When I first brought in a switch, Lynn said, "You don't have to hit them, you can sit down and talk calmly." Then somethin happened with Leah and Joshua, and Larry was tryin to talk calmly. Lynn said the next thing she saw was his belt comin off.

It kills the grandmother. She doesn't believe in switches, but I don't care. She doesn't have to take care of em, I do. When I started here, Lynn said, "Minnie, my in-laws are very prejudiced."

I said, "It doesn't bother me—she's old, and she's set in her ways." She was the type—black is black, and white is white, and this is it. I like her in spite of herself—and she's not gonna bother me; I'm not gonna bother her. Now I'm her friend.

One day she says to me, "I wish my two daughters had a Minnie to work for them."

And I said to Lynn, "You know, I think she likes me in spite of herself."

One time she said, "Everybody yells at me; everybody's mean to me, except Minnie."

I don't yell at her—I don't say anything. She's old, and if she says somethin that annoy me, I just don't pay her any attention.

Like what happened today—Sara's gonna start Hebrew school, and they were formin a car pool where I would drive for Lynn's turn. But this mornin Lynn was tellin me that she was kicked out. Lynn said that this lady down the street said she's been with this car pool before—and her housekeeper was drivin, and somebody complained. Lynn thinks she knows the person behind it, but I've had this lady's kid in my Brownie troop for two years, and she knows me—so I don't know whether it was her that complained, or somebody else. So I said to Lynn, "Well, that don't bother me at all because I'm not really anxious to drive those kids." I would do it, you know—like when Lynn and Larry's away, I drive whatever car pool they're in, and we never have any problems. But I'm not really dyin to go drivin the kids—so it won't bother me. I really didn't feel insulted. That's what killed Lynn—that I really didn't care. But the only thing that bothers me is if it involves Leah—like when the grandmother used to treat her prejudicewise. *That* used to turn me off. Now if it had been a car pool where Leah was involved, and they said, "I don't want her in it"—then I would have been upset. But to me, I guess I can blow it off—it really didn't bother me. I figure their kids the ones got to get to Hebrew school, not mine. If they don't want me to drive, I'll be happy not to drive. I figure it's Lynn's thing to work out, and she's just different—her temperament, she gets excited over nothing.

Tonight I'll probably end up stayin overnight. They're goin to a concert in the city, so I'll stay with the kids. Leah spends her days here and a lotta nights. She and Sara shares the same room. There's a bed in there that's Leah's bed–it's her bed; it was bought for her, and that's it. And the funny thing was, Lynn said Leah used to come here and go straight into the room and look at her bed—like she was checkin to see if somebody had slept in it or somethin. I didn't know it, but Lynn used to notice it. Leah doesn't mind now if somebody comes over to spend the night on the weekend. She won't say, "Better not sleep in my bed!" But Lynn used to watch her, and she'd think that Leah was really checkin to see if somebody had been there.

I have to tell you one thing that happened yesterday. Lynn had a conference with Sara's teacher—and the teacher said she was astonished when she met Leah because Sara was sayin, "I have a brother named Joshua, and a sister named Leah." So Sara's teacher didn't realize Leah was black until she finally met her. She was really surprised.

The three kids are all close, but sometimes I think Joshua and Leah might be closer. They fight a lot, they're always arguing—but there are times, you know, when the two of them will go outside and play together, and you look, and they're having a nice conversation like human beings. You can't guess em. Leah and Sara are close, but Sara's more ladylike—she's really growin up. And Leah and Joshua are still at the wild stage—they'll try anything; I mean anything!

Joshua and Leah was gonna get married one time. I said, "That's all I need—to raise my own son-in-law!"

And Lynn says, "That's all I need—Larry's mother will die!"

And that's the way we leave it. Now, they're not gonna marry each other, cause Joshua found himself a girlfriend, and Leah just went through about four boyfriends. But at one point they were gonna get married and have babies—oh, and Joshua was gonna marry me at one time, way back around the end of nursery school. The reason he isn't gonna marry me anymore was one day I said I wasn't gonna have any more babies. A few days later he said somethin about not wanting to marry me. I said, "I thought you was gonna marry me?"

He said, "You don't want any more babies, Minnie."

I said, "You're right—I sure don't!" So that was the end of marryin me.

Joshua loves to come down and visit my apartment. He always wanted to spend the night, but usually I'm not goin straight home—I'm off doin something. But he finally spent the night this summer—it was just he and Leah here. We had dinner out and everything—come back here, and he got up the next day and went home about noon. He said, "Minnie, it was really nice spendin the night in your house."

I said, "Thank you, but you slept the whole time; you really didn't do anything." So now Sara's carryin on—when is she goin to spend the night?

They love to come down and go to church with me. On Sunday I go to my Sunday school and take them to their Sunday school; then I pick em up to go back to church. And everybody knows them—they call em my kids. I'll go in sometime, they'll say, "Where's Joshua?"—cause he's always with me. We had our Minister's Banquet this year—Joshua was there. And he will take a part, you know. The way these kids have been raised—they don't feel awkward being in a church where they're the only white kids. The other kids in the church know Joshua and Sara—they play with em, they get along.

Where we go to church and where I have my apartment, there's a few whites and a lotta blacks, so Leah come in contact with the blacks. But she can't stand any of the kids down there in our neighborhood. Most of her friends have been kids in her class in school, and they've all been white. Sometime we're home on Saturdays, and she won't even go outside. She'll sit inside and pull all her toys out and play. I'll say, "Why don't you go out and play?"

"I don't want to!"

I'll say, "Why don't you invite some of your friends over?"

"I don't want em over!"

Some of em come to the door and say, "Leah, you wanta come out?"

"No!"

She goes through these things. She's a very—make up my own mind, do what I wanta do, this is it.

One time we talked about Leah growin up. Lynn says to me, "You may as well be set to it that Leah could end up marryin a white guy."

I said, "As long as they don't live with me!"

I mean, she marry a black guy—I still don't want em livin with me.

But marryin a white guy—I don't think it would trouble me. It's her life, and I have to think like that cause there's a lotta changes.

Last year we all went to Sun Valley and Jackson Hole to ski. Leah loved it. I figured that's good—she's young, she enjoys it, maybe she'll learn. I kinda did my own thing. Jackson Hole—I told em I'd never go there again. There's nothin to do. I saw the place and that's enough. I don't think I saw another black person out at Jackson Hole. I'm sure people must've seen me and figured, "Where this black lady come from?" I didn't see one black person. Not even workin at the place—that's what got me. We went into town on Saturday—I didn't see anybody. I said, "I'm sure there must be some black people there somewhere. In Wyoming there isn't any black people?" Not even walkin the streets—I didn't see not one. I said to Lynn, "There must be *somewhere* where the black people live out here." She didn't know any more than I did. I don't think Leah cared one way or the other. She told somebody she was Jewish, so you know how she feels. She's a riot.

Lynn says to me that when we come back from the trip, they went to visit a friend's house one night. There was other people there, and they were talkin about the trip. Somebody said, "You took your housekeeper to Sun Valley?"

And Lynn said, "You don't understand. Minnie's not a housekeeper, she's part of the family."

So Larry says, "Yes, on Monday she carpools; on Tuesday she bowls; on Wednesday she has choir rehearsal; on Thursday she cleans every other week; and on Friday she has Shabbos." Everybody cracked up—you know, cause on Fridays they have their Friday night dinner, the works. Lynn said everybody was rollin.

Now I bowl Friday nights, but Leah and I used to have Friday night dinner with them. And Leah learned the prayers—whatever one Sara does, she learned it too. Somebody once was talkin to her and she says, "I'm Jewish!"

So then they says, "Well, Santa Claus won't come for you—you have Hanukkah."

So then she says, "I'm half Jewish and half black."

She goes to temple with em for Yom Kippur and all that, and she loves it; she must enjoy sittin there.

When we do stay for dinner, everybody eats together, and if Lynn's friends come, I sit down to dinner with them too. In fact, Lynn's harpin about me goin to her friends' house for dinner tomorrow night—and if I don't bowl, I'll go. These friends are just like the family. If they walked in here—"Hi, Minnie, where you been?" If I go over there—"Why aren't you in the pool?" I don't swim, that's why. They're really nice, most of their friends. I guess I feel close to them. I been knowin them ever since I've been workin here. If someone calls and says to Lynn, "Can you come Friday?" I know I can come if I want. A lotta times I don't like to sit down to dinner with them, cause when I sit down, I eat and get finished and get up. They sit there and talk, and I feel like a jerk to eat so fast.

Lynn and Larry have met all my closest friends—they've met Hazel and Lorraine, and they've met Leona—my closest friends as far as girls are concerned. And when I started workin for Lynn, I was dating Leah's father—he used to always come here. Now we're not so close anymore. I have a habit of datin men too long—that's the whole trouble. Sometime I talk to myself—I say, "Minnie, you gotta start thinkin about yourself." All these years—I knew there was no future with me and Leah's father. I mean, we were seein each other—it was nice to be with him, and I didn't feel obligated—but I must have had the feelin of not wantin to hurt him. The only guy I dated after that is George, who I've been datin the last five months. Lynn's met him a lot. Larry has never met him, but when he calls on the phone, the kids get on—"George, is this you?"

If Lynn had a private party, I don't know if George would be comfortable. Leah's father, he would come in a minute—he's that type of person. But George—I keep feelin around, you know. When I was over here one afternoon, I said to him on the phone, "You could come over here."

He said somethin about, "I have to wait till you get home."

So I said, "You can come here, you know." But he never would come. So I think he has—I can't really put my finger on it, but you know there are some of us who are uncomfortable in certain situations.

Lynn says to me when I started datin George, "Are you gettin married?"

I said, "Give me one good reason why I should get married, just one. I's livin all right. I have a comfortable apartment, and I'm slowly but surely puttin in it what I want—a little bit at a time. I have a car to drive when I get ready. I have all the coverage I need—my doctor bill, insurance, and all that—Larry's taken care of it all. Now you tell me one reason to get married."

She said, "For companionship!"

"There ain't that much companion in the world!"

I don't know why I never got married. I guess if I met somebody who really just turned my head, I'd marry him. I don't know, it would have to happen first—but I'd probably be dumb enough to marry him. But now, I find all my girlfriends, the closest ones, none of us are married. Everyone's livin really independent—doin their thing, gettin along. I'm comfortable, and I guess I'm happy. People that grew up with me down in South Carolina, they have five and six kids, and their husband is livin with some other lady. To me it's just a sad situation.

Not long ago, I told Lynn, "When the kids finish high school, I'm gonna retire—I'm gonna sit down and enjoy my old age."

She says, "You can't leave me then—that's when I'll need you."

I said, "I'm not gonna sit here to hold your hand."

She said, "We're gonna hold each other's hand."

But when I retire, I'll go to my apartment and stay around there. I don't know—every time I go South peoples are doin better—nice homes and all. I keep sayin, "If I hit the million-dollar lottery, I'm goin to South Carolina." I'm sure I would miss everyone here, but I've spent half of my life here in New York. I don't do that much here, but I love bowlin— that's my big thing. And down there they don't even have a bowlin alley. Charlotte—I think that's the closest one to us. Can you imagine me driving to Charlotte to bowl? I want to keep bowlin wherever I go. I would like to go for a one-seventy average this season—I'd like to feel I'm improvin. I don't see me bowlin seven years and gettin worse, you know. Like yesterday I went and bowled, and I really didn't bowl that well. But I bowled my average—so long as I bowl my average, I'm happy. I figure, at least I'm doin what I'm supposed to.

Eva McQuay

THE FIRST TIME I SAW EVA MCQUAY WAS WHEN SHE STOOD UP TO SPEAK AT the annual luncheon meeting of the Professional Household Workers of America. There were household workers there from many of the northeastern states, as well as representatives from as far off as Ohio and North Carolina—working women who arranged their days off for this meeting, traveling at their own expense and arriving groggy from all-night bus rides, full of pride at making their presence known. The scheduled speakers were either skilled union organizers or grass-roots political leaders. They all had useful things to say, and they spoke with a simple candor that their audience appreciated. But after an hour the women began to fidget, and a few eyelids began to flutter. That was when Eva rose from her seat and began to talk. She has a gravelly voice, which she keeps at nearly full volume, as if most of her days had been spent among the deaf. She began by apologizing for having nothing to say, but, she added, she wanted to share with everyone the joy she felt at seeing household workers gathered together like this; how wonderful to think that women, exhausted from their labors, had managed to come from as far away as Columbus and Fayetteville. And didn't everyone there know that tens of thousands of families depend on household workers, couldn't get through the day without them, that a good household worker is worth her weight in gold—cook, baby-sitter, laundress, tailor, and psychiatrist rolled into one. And on and on she went. The women came to life, responding with warm laughter and interrupting with "That's right!" "Tell it!" and an occasional "Amen!" Eva is a gifted speaker, and her words come straight from felt experience.

The first time I interviewed Eva was in the Household Workers' Clothing Shop, which she founded. It wasn't much—a run-down little hole in the wall in Harlem with peeling walls and no heat—but Eva was certain that she and her fellow household workers could pool their skills and make a great success of it. Then, during the blackout of July 13, 1977, looters tore the place apart, leaving nothing. Months of planning and fund-raising, hundreds of hours of work, were completely destroyed. When I saw Eva again in September, she'd set up a new shop in a more secure building and thrown a big block party to get things moving. She was brimming with plans once again.

My name is Eva Belle McQuay. I was born June the fifth, 1918, in a place called Arcadia, Florida—better known as Cowtown because there were a lotta rodeos and whatnot then. Durin the epidemic of the flu, round in 1917 I think it was, my mother had children about six years old, and five, but the flu came through and all her children died. I understand people would be up in the mornin and they would die by nighttime because the flu was just that bad. In Jacksonville they started hangin up pieces of beef to catch the fever, and they said by noontime the beef would be fallin off the bone—the fever in the air was that intense. People was just dyin like flies. I was the first born after my mother lost her children.

My mother and father had a farm, and he kept a group of men workin, hewin out these seven-by-nine cross-ties for the railroad company, which netted him a pretty good sum. My family was—considered like what it is now—you would have five hundred dollars in the bank, well you considered whatchya call a bourgeois black, you know. As a child I didn't know anything about housework. My father always had trucks and men workin, but the depression came along and it knocked out everything. And I think that was the reason for his death—he never did get over it.

So after that, well we had to try to survive, you know. My mother started doin washin and ironin, and I started baby-sittin for a quarter, and we came along like that. I was always lucky. I was so good in home economics, I won a scholarship to go out to California, but my mother wouldn't dare let me go. She said that was too far from home, and when my father passed, the home was just halfway finished payin for, so somebody had to stay to help her face the bills. So my mother took in washin and ironin. You know, fifty cents made for a little bit. And for a wagonload, what we would get twenty-five dollars for now, she only got a dollar and a half. We had big washpots, and you had to pump your water. My mother made her own soap in the backyard outa lye. It was very difficult in those days. You had to put your irons on an old coal bucket to heat them—and you really could do some nice ironin, no kiddin. And when you get able enough to buy a gas iron for six dollars and somethin, you was really called a highfallutin person.

Workin around white folks we got lotsa respect. But the thing about it—you knew your place, and you stayed in your place. My mother told me, "Don't let your hands stick to nothin in those peoples' houses, and don't be eatin things unless they give it to you, and don't you bring nothin home unless they give it to you! And it's 'Yes, ma'am' and 'No, ma'am.'" I never will forget. When my daddy was livin, somehow or another they all liked him, and he always had as much money as he wanted. He could jus go to his boss and say, "Look, I want five hundred dollars."

"Well, ole darkie"—that's what they used to call him—"Ole darkie, all right, here it is."

That was the president of the bank. You see, in that time my father thought that was a great honor—to be called an old darkie. It made them feel like they were wanted. Really, you'd be surprised.

Around that time I did some dress designin. I always wanted to be a dress designer—I guess so, because when I was little, I cut up all my mother's things. One time I was with my sister, and I done cut somethin with a hole in it and hung it over her head. She's modelin it—it was somethin she really wanted—and my mother came in. But she wouldn't strap me about that too much, she really wouldn't—she would just raise the devil. And along in that time, in the high school I always made A's and B's, and I would make dresses for the other kids, and they would give me ten cents. So that kept me with money in my pocket all the time—and see, the thing about it is when they came outa school they couldn't sew, and I could. That's what happens to a lotta people—they get somebody else to do their work, and when it comes down to the nitty-gritty of the thing, they just don't know.

When the depression come, there was the—whatchya call it?—the BRA, WPA—and I got a chance to work on the playgrounds with kids. I got six dollars a month plus I would baby-sit and plus our washin—and Momma would raise our garden in the back and sell the eggs and chickens. So that's how we made it through. And I always kept a little shop goin, always hemmin up somethin for somebody. Didn't get but fifty cents for a dress. Long in that time you could buy calico for five cents a yard or ten cents a yard. Somebody comes on Saturday morning, and they want a dress to wear Sunday morning—and that's what they wore to church. You didn't wear silk or anything too much like that. And you starched your dress, and you'd iron it till it almost stand up by itself. You'd put it on—you could hear it rattle like that. And petticoats, the petticoats would ruffle—oh, it was just so pretty! The petticoat would be stiff, you know, just ironed and standin out, and the dress over it. Whenever a lady kind of stooped or somethin or other, you could see it just looked so pretty. They don't treasure that kind of stuff now. The ladies was very feminine round in that time. They used to wear long blouses with the ruffle come out here starched stiff, and they had something in the front called a jabot. When the lady's breathing, that jabot'd jus be movin up and down like that—couldn't breathe deeply cause you tied up so tight. And they'd put on the girdle—I remember when Momma would fall out puttin the girdle on, and Daddy would laugh hisself to death cause we had to string her up in the back and tie her, and she'd say, "I have to breathe!"

I got married to an old guy round then. He was a shoe man. He finished at Tuskeegee, and he was an orthopedic—you know, that made these special shoes. Well, he worked in a shoe shop, and he got paid pretty good for that. He was too old to go over in the army, so they sent him home to me. And he cleaned buildings over at Florida Power and Light, and he cleaned the big national bank, you know, shine all the brass and the knobs at night. So that made him get along pretty good. No children. The doctor said they couldn't pin me down long enough to have a kid. So that's it. Well, at that time I was earnin a little check and tryin to get rich, but I come down with something called phlebitis and they said I'd never walk. I had a time—I was just as big and fat as could be, and couldn't walk a step. They did everything. They had a old straw-bottomed chair, and they put a bucket of boiling water under there with steam comin up, and they put a wool blanket around me, and, oh boy, I just sweat, the water just rolled off me! They'd stand me up, and I'd holler like somebody was killin me—look like I was leavin. So they made me drunk—somethin I didn't do—tryin to get me loosened up. For days I couldn't pick my feet up—they just looked like they was too heavy. But I hollered and I cried, and after two years I finally learned to walk—I had to learn all over again.

You know, back there they had what you call seasonal work. All through my younger days I knew people would come through the North, like Maine and different places, and they'd work the seasons. When they stayed the whole season, they would get bonuses, and that's what made you live like a big shot when you get back home. In Florida, when the oranges all finished and that kinda thing, it was kinda hard, so I did farm work in New York for a few seasons. Northern people always had some black person that stands out to get the recruitin done. So when the season is going down, you say, "Well, here is Mr. So-and-So, he's gettin up a bus."

Well, somebody else say, "I don't wanta go with him. I went with him last year—it wasn't so good."

And this one over here says, "Well, I'm goin with him. I hear he's got good propositions."

You know, people discuss this. And when it comes time, he'll come around and ask who's goin, take your name and everything. When it comes the day, the buses all come, you load your little junk in, and you get on over there and stay the season. It's a long ride. You're tired and you got your lunches. When you're ready to eat, they'll stop along the road and you'll get a bunch of sodas—just so you didn't go in the front of the store. Go in the back door and get all you could buy, spend all the money you have—but you couldn't go in the front. You'd expect this, so you didn't care nothin. You goin to make some money, cause there's no money where you're at—so you're not kickin up no sand. You don't have no bread where you're at, so you're goin where some bread is. And you're comin back with money in your pocket. You understand?

You got along fine up North because you was with your own gang.

That's why they sent for you—they didn't have nobody of their own to do the work. When you get there, they have this government camp, you know, where the soldiers had been. Then you're assigned to your room—have your blankets, your cot, and whatnot. In the mornin, when they ring the bell, everybody comes to the post. They had different places you could go—you could go to the field to pull grass, you could go to pick tomatoes, you could go to pick peaches, you could pick sweet peas, or you could go to the plant to can the food.

The plant, it runs twenty-four hours. The big belt, man, you see the food comin down on that belt! Somebody see a big green worm—he's standin up there and you can't even reach him, and the ladies is all in line pullin off the rotten food and everything—and sometimes the ole worm just go right on down the line, and come on down and gets in a little box. The girls puts the box on the scale and weigh it to make sure that you have the right amount of poundage in there, and it falls down in a little slot. Oh, the worm's in there, wherever he is—and this machine'll seal it up just like—you see how beautiful they seal it up? They seal it, and it goes and the man loads em on his dolly and carries em on down somewhere where it's so many degrees below, and it freezes for awhile, and the trucks is out there, and they're loadin boxes on the trucks—catchin them, just dancin like little fairy dolls or something goin round. It goes on all the twenty-four hours.

At night there wasn't nothin for you to do but go to bed and be around your own campfire. You know, these small towns, they didn't have no dance halls and nightclubs. There was nothin to do after you go to the field all day but find a place where you could get washed up—an old tub or somethin. You didn't go nowhere—you just told jokes and went from one room to the other. You didn't think about goin up into town, cause it was hilly—you tired, you didn't want to climb the hills. Well, the ones that drank beer and stuff, maybe at night just one or two guys would go up to get the stuff, and everybody'd chip in. They'd bring it back down and drink it—"Well, I went last night. Your turn, So-and-So."

Then on Saturday night the band would come out from the city, and they'd have big dances. People would come out from the city because they wanta play poker. You'd be surprised what go on. The sharks, they'd come from the city and take away these poor southerners' money—they don't know how to gamble too good, that's what these sharks lookin for. On Sunday they would have a bus come out. Everything is fixed for you. You get on the bus, you go into Canada. If you stayed in the South, you would never get a chance to do this—to go into Canada and look. And next Sunday maybe you go into a different place—until you get ready to go back South, go back home.

Then around 1950 I began doin housework. This lady recommended me to a friend in New York, and she was gonna give me thirty-five dollars a week. Well, that's great! I can't get that. And I hear after you get there you can make even more money than that. That was money! I always wanted to come to New York, but my momma wouldn't let me. I had to do what she said—"You not comin to New York." All my friends would come, and they would get things, and they would be sendin them home to the ones that was less fortunate and everything. And now I wanted some of the cake—so when this woman offered me thirty-five dollars, I got my little self together and I come to New York. What I brought with me? That's my trouble, because everywhere I ever went I always got a load of stuff. My momma always taught me—even when I go to my brother's house—I carry my own washcloth, I carry my soap; I don't care what you got there, I got my towel. I come to my brother's, hang my own towel on the hall rack. Oh, he gets angry. And my momma always told me a woman oughta always have a set of sheets and things of her own. I don't care where you're at, you oughta have some linen of your own. I was just brought up like that. So I got my load of stuff together and come on up here to this little building around Eighty-sixth Street on the West Side.

When I was home in the South, I always pictured New York was a place where people'd come, and you just could get the money, and everybody was dressed up, and you just didn't see dirty people and nappy lookin people and all this kinda stuff, you know. And when I came and got a chance to get down in Harlem and really see dirty people, I just didn't hardly know what to think. The way I got to Harlem—I was brought up on collard greens, chittlins, hog maws, and pig tails, and see, up there on Eighty-sixth Street I didn't see any of that kinda thing. They had what you call cottage cheese and all this kinda stuff. I was starvin to death, and man, I got in a cab to get me somethin I could eat. And by some hook or crook, the guy that was drivin the cab was a boy—his father worked for my daddy when he was cuttin the seven-by-nine ties. So when I got in there and sits back, he says, "Eva Belle McQuay!"

I look around; I say, "Busby! Wow, what is this!" That was really somethin.

He said, "How ya doin?"

I said, "Man, I'm hungry! Can you tell me a place where I can get some collard greens?"

He carried me down—I never will forget it—down near the Eighth Avenue parta Harlem. And ever since, I was goin down there to get myself some collard greens, cause I couldn't get nothin like that up there. Oh, I was starvin!

Well now, I worked for that thirty-five dollars a week until I found some more of my friends was makin bigger money than I was makin. Well, you know people would get together and want to know what you do— "What she have you to do? What you make?"

"I don't get but thirty-five dollars."

"That's all you gettin is thirty-five dollars?"

I'd say, "Yeah, man!"

"Oooh, you workin for nothin! You crazy!"

Now when I go back home, when I go back to my little bunk that I'm sleepin on—I'm not happy now. I'm thinkin, "Oh, this woman brought me up here, and she's makin somethin on me." So now every week when I come uptown, my friends keep callin me a fool. Well, you know I don't want nobody to keep tellin me I'm stupid and this and that—I get unhappy, and I don't wanta stay in my job. So now—I never will forget it—there was a agency right down here called the Hudson, or somethin or other like that. I went in there and I told the woman I wanted a job. She said, "Well, I got a Miss Roth, she lives out here on a Hundred Sixty-first Street. I'm gonna tell you right now, she's hard to please but she pays good money."

I said, "How much she pays?"

"She pays fifty dollars a week."

Oh, I didn't care what she had there to do. It didn't make no difference to me. She's payin fifty dollars.

So I went on out to Miss Roth's house. That day she had people comin in and out to interview—just like they was goin in and out of a field or somethin. So I stayed on the outside and waited my turn. She'd take em in one by one—oh, she was somethin all right. So when I gets in there, she looks at me, she says, "Can you make a hollandaise sauce?"

I said, "What's that?" You see, southern people didn't make all that fancy sauce to put on the broccoli. You just put a little mayonnaise on, or you took a little catsup and mayonnaise or somethin—that's all you did.

So she said, "You mean to tell me you cook, and you, you can't——"

I says, "No."

But I was smart. When I come to New York, I bought me a big cookbook for three ninety-eight—you could get some kinda cookbook for three ninety-eight. So I had my cookbook with me—I always go in prepared—I said, "Miss Roth, I can fix anything under the sun if you tell me how you want it and it's in this book."

She didn't hardly know what to say. She's a little old woman. Well, now, she questioned me all kinda ways—what do I know, how I live, and all this kinda stuff—and who're my people, if I'm this and I'm that. When she got through she said, "You know, I interviewed so many women that been on jobs for twenty years, and thirty years——" she saw I was a nice little pushover, and I wasn't gonna tell her no about nothin. She said, "And I didn't take those people with all that experience, but somehow I like you, and I'm gonna take you."

You know, talkin about those fancy sauces Miss Roth wanted me to make—over the years I came to see somethin surprisin about white people's food. Long time ago, our people were very poor. White people didn't know nothin but the chicken legs and the breasts, and we ate the backs and wings and chicken livers—all this kinda stuff. Way back that time, you could go to the market on Saturday—the man'd give you those kinda things free; you didn't even have to buy them. But as the years rolled on, white people started eatin our food and callin it by fancy names. Now you take the chicken wings, you fix em up nice and brown—it's an hors d'oeuvre, and boy, you gonna pay for it too, when you go to one of them parties. Chicken livers? You can't find a better hors d'oeuvre than chicken livers with crackers and whatnot—chopped livers. And my mammy, she usedta buy milk, take the cream off, make the butter, let the milk sour, and then we'd make clabbered milk. She'd beat it up and put sugar or syrup in it, and we ate it. Now they got it all dressed up—now it's yogurt; it's good for reducin, it's good for this, it's good for that. Oh, they got fancy French names of all kind! Listen, they fix up the foods all kinda fantastic ways, I'm tellin you, and when you see these names, you wonder what it is. I went somewhere to eat somethin. I see "quiche"—what in the devil is that? I didn't want to—you know, sometime you think you appear real stupid to ask some questions. So I order it and then find out my mother had been cookin it all my life. Momma would stir up eggs with onions and all that kinda stuff. She didn't put it in a crust—she just stir it up and whatnot. "All right, hold your plate over here!" Thap! "Hold your plate over there!" Thap! And she'd just serve it like that. Now they put it in a crust—a quiche. All the southern people, they cooked all those things, you know, a long time ago. They just cooked em, didn't have no special names.

But now gettin back to Miss Roth—she damn near killed me. I didn't have a day off, but I didn't care nothin about that because I was gettin the fifty dollars. But what ruined it—after she got done hirin me she said, "Listen, I will not pay you fifty dollars. I will only pay you forty-five dollars cause you're not experienced, and when you're experienced I'll pay you the fifty dollars." Well, I done left the other job, and this was still more than the thirty-five dollars. Well, I worked! Man, she'd go out to the restaurant, she'd get all kinda cookin recipes—I didn't have time for nothin. She'd call up from downtown somewhere and say, "You put another plate to the table, put two more plates, I got some friends here." Man, inside of a week or two I was cookin anything you wanted to name. She went somewhere and got a thing called zabay-baloney or somethin—you eat it like a pudding and put wine in it—yeah, zabaglione, that's it! She'd have me makin cookies in the evenin and baggin em up for her friends that came over from Scarsdale. Well now, I got mad cause it was just too much. I didn't have no time off. And if her friend would give a dinner party, she'd take me along—"There may be somethin you can help or do. Come on, you goin with us to the dinner, too." No time to even read the paper.

Then she'd keep me dancin with her shoppin. She'd go to Lord and Taylor and buy one or two things; then she'd go to Saks—she had a credit for every one of em. You put the children on the bus in the mornin, and someone's at the front door.

"Who's this?"

"A package for Roth——" You get it and bring it in the house. Before you can get back to the kitchen and put anything down or whatnot—rrring, the bell goes again.

"Who's it?"

"Saks Fifth Avenue. I got a package." You can't get nothing done.

Now after she got all her clothes delivered, she'll have a night, put on these things so that her husband decide what he want and what he don't want. One night I was so glad I had to laugh. Remember when they started to wear rhinestones on their dresses? Well, she bought this gingham dress, and it had a rhinestone on just about every dot in the little square. That was a hundred ninety-five dollars or somethin. She put that on and walked into the foyer. The old man—he was kinda an old man, like—he asked her how much it was.

"I'll be damned if I'll pay!" he said.

I was so glad, man, I was in the kitchen laughin.

He said, "I will not pay for it!"

She didn't argue with him. Well now, she put on all these things, and then she'd pack em up. "All right, Eva, this goes back to Macy's, this goes back to Saks."

So now the doorbell rings. "Hello who is that?"

"This is Macy's, I come for a pickup." Now you started gettin em back out, right back out. She's not home to do anything. You just start in runnin with your tongue hangin out. I'm tellin you. That was one house job—I think that paid off for everything else.

So then I came down on her. I wanted my five dollar raise.

"Oh, not yet. The business is bad."

Business was bad, and this and that. My husband got hold of a job, he said, "Listen, you come on home."

Well, I said. "Miss Roth, I'm sorry but I'm goin home. I can't work for this money."

Well, she didn't believe me. I got my little money and stuff and carried everything up to this room I got for eight dollars.

She called me up. "What's the matter, Eva?"

"Well, I'm goin over to another job, Miss Roth, for more money, cause I need more money."

"Ohhhh, money is what's wrong with you. Why didn't you tell me. Money is no hardship—come here, come quick, you got to come here."

I go there, she's sittin down cryin, tears comin away. She knew I couldn't stand to see her cry. She give me ten dollars more, but oh, did I pay for it—oh my God! She got ready to move to Scarsdale—she built a home out there.

So I say, "Miss Roth, I can't go to Scarsdale. I got to go home on vacation first."

"Well, all right, all right, you go. I won't pack nothin till you get back."

I says, "All right."

"But Eva, I can't pay you a full vacation pay. You go and you come back, and I'll give you the pay when you get back."

I ain't never got that vacation pay cause I never did go back.

Of course, not all the jobs are like that. But that's why we're tryin to upgrade the profession—because household workers, they're looked down on as nobody. And believe me, what they do is skill, because when you take care of somebody's prize possession, their children, and when you set the table in the very best manner, put everything in its respected place and everything—you can't go to school for that, you have to be skilled. You have to be skilled to know how long to cook a roast beef, or how many minutes to let a steak cook if they want it medium. If you servin different kinda wines, you have to know what glass you use. It's really a profession; it's really skill, cause some people can't even cook a decent egg for you to eat. You know, it's somethin when you've got to tell a person everything you want done, but when you've got a person in your house, a person you don't have to tell what to do, and you can rest assured that it's done—it's really worth every penny of it. And a person wouldn't be able to go out and make that big money if they couldn't find a household worker to come in and do their work. It's a blessin to come into the house and your food is all fixed, your house is all clean; if you havin company everything is all set up and ready to go—you have no worries. Well look, you have to pay for it—same thing you pay other workers. What we're fightin for nowadays—we's human beings, we need to rest too sometimes, we'd like to have a little vacation. And you fall in the house and break your hip or anything like that—listen, there's no insurance or anything. You haven't made enough money or saved enough money to pay the doctor bills, because the doctor bills now is just outa sight. So somethin have to be done.

You learn this though—when you tell them you goin home and they know they can't take care of that house, they gonna do somethin to get you to come back. They can't take on all that—can you just imagine when you've got two or three bad children? You got to get em dressed, you got to get em out to school, and they tearin up and rippin and tearin. And the husband, he's lookin at you cross-eyed, he wants you to do this, he wants you to tend to this, and here you got the kids. Maybe this one's sittin at the table and he won't eat, and you have to sit there, you stick the food at him and do the bird—"Eeeeat! Open your mouth up; here comes the bird." Bam! Get it in there fast. Do the bird, any kinda thing to make them eat. Poor woman ain't got time for all that kinda stuff—the maid gotta do that, you know. Oh, it's really a riot when you come to think of it. That old man is fussin; the button done jumped off his shirt—the poor woman didn't have time, and maybe she's a little old delicate thing; can't do too much nohow—and then the shirt is all dirty, and probably he's got to go to the office. He can't go there lookin all kinda way. And probably she's in one or two organizations, she have to be there to keep herself up in the community, so her friends won't be talkin—"You know, Susie don't go nowhere, that man has got her down there—" you'd be surprised how people talk. You got to keep up your social side, your every side. And let me tell you, if you got it all to do yourself, it's not funny. And when you got a household worker in your house that can do everything, and you don't have to get frustrated and everything, it's just a jewel in there, it really is. And you can tell all the jewels because they've been there twenty-five and thirty years and them people is not about to let them go either. You can believe that.

And then I say this—you know a long time ago you used to call the help "mammies." Sometimes the mistress would put all her faith—if Mammy said it, that was it; they had that much respect. Well, I remember one night I was workin. The husband and the mistress—I ain't supposed to know nothin—they had a little argument. He musta looked at a little old gal or somethin, and she got all—oh man, she was pitchin things. He jumped in the car and he went flyin, and she came runnin to the kitchen to me—"Eva, he's gone, he's gone."

I say, "Oh, he ain't goin nowhere. Listen, he's just goin right round the corner and he'll be back. He's got to cool off. You go on in there and dress up for your dinner party, and I'll fix dinner."

"I thought maybe we shouldn't have the dinner."

I said, "No, let the dinner roll!"

After awhile they all sittin up at the table. She's sittin up there like a little mouse, you know, she don't know what to do. He comes in, take off his overcoat and everything, and come and sit down at the table lookin like one of them mummies. Nobody say nothin about the fight. See what I'm talkin about? Back in the kitchen with me, she didn't know what to do. If she'd of stopped the dinner from goin on, that woulda made it worse. She had company comin, the dinner's bein fixed—well, what else?—let the dinner roll, he'll be back. She needed somebody to tell her somethin right quickly. She didn't know what to do. You'd be surprised how people have to do thinkin for another. Like Miss Roosevelt when her husband was president—sometime you see a person holdin these big jobs, and you'd be surprised who's standin behind tellin them what to do and how to run this thing and get it over. They just there in the body, but somebody is feedin the coals to the fire.

Now after I worked so long, I was makin this tremendous salary, and my foot all swolled up again. I says, "Oh, I can't go it no longer." So I went into a paint factory for seventy-five cents an hour. I dropped down from this nice salary to seventy-five cents an hour—and they take out everything. I got around twenty-eight dollars a week. For years I worked in those paints—mixin colors and sprayin—and they went into my system. I had about five operations—they had to cut me, take out a piece of my liver; then I got a hernia, and then I got a thyroid tumor. Oh, I just got everything. I went back in the hospital and stayed a year, and when I come out I wasn't fit for nothin.

One day this social worker come to me and says, "Listen, we oughta do somethin with you. Maybe we could rehabilitate you."

I says, "How in the world can you rehabilitate me, and I got to stay in the bathroom all the time?"

Well, she left me alone, she didn't bother me no more cause I told her the truth. Then I met a girl called Eudora Moll, she say, "Eva, don't you wanta go to Washington? They havin a trip down there for household workers, and they doin this, they doin that."

I say, "Eudora, I just come outa the hospital. I can't stand to ride—it look like the shakin from the bus'll bother me on the inside. I can't go."

Geraldine Miller, she was the founder that got the bus from the Urban League and everything. Well, when they got on down the road and organized, I got in there. They wanted to know how they could get members. Well, I said, "Nobody wants to join a dead wagon. You've got to do somethin to entice people to come in here. You can't just tell people to come in here—and here's a bunch of leaders sittin up barkin about household workers and all this stuff. You've gotta do somethin. You know what'd be a good thing for household workers to do? Why don't they get together and make uniforms? Everybody wears uniforms—and they could do this, we could start a business." Well, everybody thought it was a good idea. We got the thing incorporated.

Well, now we shimmyin on down the road here—I said, "Well, why don't we just start a sewin class?" We got a sewin class, got it goin now about three years down at the Church of Intercession. People been comin and goin—we turn out some very good students there.

Come up again to raise some money, so I said, "You know what we could do, we could have the community to participate, and let retired household workers knit hats, knit gloves, and do this, and we'll sell it for them, and that'll show that we're workin in the community." Well, it was goin so good, we decided we'd make a store out of it. We didn't have no license or nothin, so we went down to the precinct. Well, the policeman down there, the head man at the precinct, he said, "Well, I'll write you out this slip here, and you go on back, and if any of the boys come by, you just show em the slip."

I said, "Now we'll have a store openin. What we'll do, we'll get all the big celebrities and politicians, and all this kinda stuff, and see what we can do."

At that time, Bella [Abzug] was doin her campaign—I was down there lickin stamps and closin up envelopes and this kinda stuff. And we'd just had a big benefit at Carolyn Reed's house for Mary Anne Krupsak—so we showin up. I come here and made a Big Apple pillow outa velvet and embroidered BELLA all over it. Oh boy! So now when we called on them, they can't reneg! Boy, we had a big get-together over there. Some of the household workers made nearly a hundred dollars with the stuff they made, and that's what give us the kickoff.

Then we got up a committee of domestic workers—the Committee of Twelve, we called it. I looked at this thing, I says, "Now look here, everybody's a household worker. Even if you married and got a husband, you gotta do the housework. You don't wanta say it, you don't wanta be affiliated with it—you think it's a downgradin thing, and you make these people the last thing on the totem pole. But when you think about it, they right up on the totem pole with everybody else. The thing about household workers—they got to get off of their behinds and they got to make people recognize them. People just don't wanta give them no recognition—they don't have no fringe benefits at all; they don't get social security; they need sick leave the same as other human beings. They're human. Now see, that's what we want now—it's no more than right!"

I went to Washington not long ago, bellerin on this. And a woman out of Atlanta—Mrs. Dorothy Bolden, a leader of domestic workers—yeah, she was expoundin. Oh boy, she can talk! We was in the White House with Margaret Costanza. Oh, we was there! They took us to the Red Room, the Blue Room, and every room you could name—and we went all over the place. It was beautiful. Miss Costanza's a liaison to Carter, so she relayed our message to him. I says, "Listen, there's somethin you can do in the legislation. You don't have to spell it out, you know, that you're doin this—but in the legislation, you can let a little toppin fall down on our ice cream cone. You know what I mean? Because we're people down there—we cause the ball to roll, we the spoke in the wheel—don't forget that. You're out there, you're in your law office—I wash your shirts so you can sit up there. And then you might be pleadin my son's case, getting money from me—I'm causin you to go. I'm stayin home with your children; I'm causin you to hold this job out there to get twenty-five thousand dollars a year, or whatever it is. I'm doin your work at home—I'm answerin your telephone, I'm settin up your dinner, makin a balanced meal at night, and when you come in all you got to do is sit down. That's worth money. And I'm inclined to think that people are not gettin the minimum wage, and you don't see that it's enforced. And even the minimum wage now is not enough for a person to live out of accordin to cost-of-living standards. It causes crime. A woman goes to work, and she comes home and the son ask for a bottle of soda water, and you just only able to pay the rent—he's gonna get a bottle of soda water from somewhere. He's gonna do somethin. Children are not born to be bad, but you see other kids with things and whatnot, and you can't get it for him—he steals it. He gets into one little thing, and he goes from one thing to another. He thinks that's the right way—and you out workin for someone; you not home to teach him, and you can't find nobody to stay there because you not gettin the minimum wage. It's kinda bad."

Well, now we got some organization and there's all the activities I'm thinkin to get goin. I want an award dinner—to give out awards to everybody that contributed in the beginning of this thing. And I want a book where you sell advertisements in there for one hundred dollars a page to go along with it. But I can't have that till next year because I don't want it half-planned. Then when I get this workshop set up the way I want it,

I want to sell shares in it. But I want to be able to buy the most shares, cause I don't want nobody to come in here and control this thing after I done work so hard for these women. And I want these shops in every state, every little city. And the cookin and restaurant business should go for household workers—I want to open a restaurant where poor people can get food cheaper—Household Workers name up there on the restaurant. I like the laundry business—I wanta open up a laundromat in some city—that's Household Workers' Laundromat up there. Understand what I mean? I'd like one to have tubs and things in there, and if a woman doesn't wanta do household work and whatnot, she can come in and do hand laundry for somebody—leave it there in the mornin, iron the shirts and everythin, and you can get it that night. And for the people in the upper echelons we'll have what you call first-class boutique shops where Mrs. Rockefeller would like maybe wanta shop in. We'll have that for her too. You are furnishin a commodity—you assurin people you can promote somethin for the betterment of this world, for the betterment of human beings. This is what I see in the future. There'll be a lot of shops like this clothing shop for poor people. We've had people goin to funerals and stuff—they can't find a black dress downtown to go to a funeral. They come in here, they find a black dress, and they don't have to pay their eye for it. We look around, we find a dress that looks nice—they got it and they're gone. We'll try to have the things what other people don't have—we'll try to have them at cut-rate so we can reach the poor people. This is what the Household Workers' Workshop is all about.

You know, I guess I got a lot of religious things about me, traits and whatever, you might say, because I was brought up in the church—and you see, when Jesus Christ was goin through the world, he help a lotta people. A lotta times people come in here and they say, "I don't have this, I don't have that," and I try to give em somethin, or do something, or tell em somethin. If you don't help nobody in this world, then you just die on out; your name just gone out with you; you haven't done anything while you was here. I think you come here to contribute to the universe here; you come here to help people. Somebody is hungry—you mean to tell me you got money, and I ask you for a biscuit, and you can give me a biscuit, and you don't? I think it's a sin. I think if I could leave something here behind for the young generation to come along and profit by it—I figure, well, I didn't live here in vain, I left a footprint in the sand here.

If you don't leave nothin here, a pattern left for somebody to go by, what good is it? And then I find this—as you get older, if you don't help anybody, you don't mix with people, you don't communicate—you goes home when you get a certain age; you goes in between your four walls; nobody come in there to talk with you or inspire you; you don't inspire nobody; you grow old; you grow crabby in there by yourself; you *die* in there by yourself. If you notice all the people that were some use in this world—they always just so beautiful—they out here workin, they're doin somethin. It means somethin to you to be able to help, to be able to contribute. I like to go to meetins; I like to know what's going on. You a backwoods number if you don't mingle with people, don't come out in the world. You don't help nobody, so nobody have nothin good to say about you—"Well, he live there alone; he didn't bother nobody," that's about all. But just to come out and to know that you caused somethin to happen for a person—you don't get paid for everything you do, but somethin comes good to you some other way. That's the way I live—things come to me by little things I do.

Carolyn Reed

For the past few years Carolyn Reed has been a leader in the movement to bring household workers together and to lobby for the basic work benefits that her people need. She is always on the run—one of the few household workers to receive phone calls with an answering machine. Perhaps her most important struggle has been her fight to secure collective bargaining rights for household workers. She has appeared repeatedly before committees of the New York state legislature, explaining the needs of household workers to groups of middle-aged, middle-class white men. She has found some sympathetic listeners and a few active allies, but at this point the state legislature has only managed a compromise bill, which grants collective bargaining rights to women employed by contract cleaning firms but ignores the needs of the remaining 80 percent of household workers. And collective bargaining is merely a preliminary goal—securing basic work benefits is still a long way off.

Numerous feminist and political action groups have sought Carolyn out, as well as journalists, television interviewers, reporters, and one or two Ph.D. researchers. All of this has brought needed attention to the needs of working women, and Carolyn's frank talk has surely helped counteract the old image of the docile, easily pacified maid. Her activism has forced people to sit up and begin to take household workers seriously, but these days Carolyn is somewhat put off by easy praise, by eager journalists and organizers who want a spokesperson to represent household workers, by politicians who sympathize but do little, by researchers who want to study her people—so I have not tried to praise her, to set her up as *the* household worker, or to study her. I do want to thank her, though, for her encouragement and her friendship—and for a box lunch she gave me once. It was at the same meeting where I met Eva McQuay, and when the morning session broke up I told Carolyn I had to run off to another appointment. She handed me a box lunch and told me the fried chicken was too good to miss. Then, remembering I'd just lost my job in the City College retrenchment plan, she handed me a second box. "Here, you'd better take this one too," she said. Her mouth widened in a mischievous grin, "All of us here have work, and you're unemployed. We household workers may be poor, but we musn't forget there are people less fortunate than ourselves."

It's really funny that you start with asking who am I, because really I don't know who I am at this particular point in my life. I was born in Rockaway on November 25, 1939. I used to shock everybody and say I was a bastard—just for the shock value. My mother was in college in South Carolina, and somehow I came about. Then she came to live with her aunt up North in Rockaway, until she had me. She went—I don't know where. I haven't seen her since. That's another story in itself. Never knew my father.

I spent my first seven years with my grand-aunt in Brooklyn. She was a household worker—she worked for the same family until she retired. That's where I used to get my clothes, because the family had a daughter a little older than me. So I got what I thought was all these marvelous clothes, really fantastic things, at that point in my life. Don't never even remember seeing the people at all, even though my grand-aunt spoke fondly of them up until the time she died. I can't even remember their name.

I was kind of adopted when I was seven years old, and taken to South Carolina. I considered the South my home because I grew up there until I was sixteen. The people who took me were distant cousins of my grand-aunt. He came up to visit one summer, and my aunt said, "Do you want a little girl?" He said, "Yes," so he took me home with him—much to the dismay of his wife. I mean, he arrives off the train, and she meets him, and she's looking for him—and here comes this skinny kid along with him. He worked in a local theater as a ticket-taker—and I remember him throwing kids out if you make noise, and slipping some kids in. In the theater the blacks were upstairs and the whites were downstairs, but I never realized it was segregated because I thought we had the better seats upstairs.

I did not have a great awareness of segregation. It's funny because we lived in a black community, we played in a black community, but you sort of never felt bad about it—not until in the latter part of high school when the civil rights movement really began. I had teachers then that were marvelous—black teachers that were really interested in helping children. I always remembered something that an English teacher told me—we were just beginning to really discuss the difference between black and white, what we had and didn't have and what *they* had and didn't have—and my teacher said, "You are as good as anyone—you're just as good as anyone, but you're not better than anyone." And they sort of instilled that into us—that you can be anything that you would like to be. It helped me to develop at that time, but now that I look on it, it was certainly a damn lie. They used to always say, "You can grow up to be president." And you know that is just not true. It helped me develop in a certain way, but I don't know if I were a teacher whether I would say you can grow up to be anything you wanta be. I mean, I'm angry about it now. I was not angry about it then because I didn't know.

There was another teacher, Mr. Middleton, who was very funny because he was always talking with his hands, and he was spitting all over the place. But he used to say, "Ask questions, always ask questions. Never just take it for granted that something is true because someone tells you." And I found that's been very useful in my life. He said, "Regardless of how crazy the question may be, there's always somebody who wants to know the same thing, but they're too timid to ask it." And so, yeah, I had a marvelous education in the South—the teachers were into teaching you, really into development. The only reason that I go back to the South now is to see the teachers—it's not to see the family that raised me because I can't stay in the house more than twenty-four hours before I have another fight of some kind. I can't be what I'm not, and I refuse to go to church and stay all day.

Growing up, I was self-conscious because my adopted mother was always preaching to me that "Your mother didn't want you." That was something that I had to—to fight—and it kind of bothered me. Then one day I thought of this answer to her and sort of got it off my back. I said, "Well, my mother did not keep me because she could not afford to keep me, and she thought I was gonna go to nice people who would love me. But she loved me—that's why she gave me up." It must have been the right thing to say, because this woman just stared at me. But actually, those things bothered me more when I got older, I don't know why, but when I got married I figured that I had to introduce Ken to whatever family I had. That's when I took him down South. Of course, he just thought it was marvelous, and I told him they were putting on an act. I said, "It wasn't this way when I lived here." You know, we were greeted with open arms, and I was their long-lost daughter, and the whole thing. I couldn't stand it—I couldn't stand for her to touch me and do this whole kissing act. Listen, we'd never done that before! It was really strange. Ken said he had never seen that side of me before—a very cold side which said, "Don't touch me!" So Ken said, "Rather than be constantly having fights, why don't you just say, 'Listen, let's go our separate ways.'" Which is what I've done. We kind of came to the conclusion that I would not deal with that at all, because I can't deal with something that has so many bad memories. I'd like to sort of leave it alone.

I became involved in household work at sixteen when I came to spend the summer with my aunt in Brooklyn. I got me a *Long Island Press* and decided that I'd get a job as a mother's helper. I lied and said I was eighteen or some crazy age. I got this job in East Meadow, Long Island, and felt very independent with being able to take care of myself. At long last, I was supporting myself and did not have to rely on anyone. Back South I used to pick up and dust for our school principal—we called him

Professor—and do a little hand washing. I made something like five bucks a week, which I felt was a hell of a lot of money. But East Meadow was the first real job that I'd ever had. They had this marvelous house—they were rich. I guess I felt a little self-conscious, but I got my act together because I knew that there were a couple of lies I had to tell. They said for me to help with the cooking—I never cooked before in my life; I'd never been allowed in the kitchen. But I knew I could read, and I figured I could follow a recipe, so I brought along a cookbook with me. I'd never been with children before, because I grew up as an only child and I just never had known anything about changing a baby's diaper—but I figured that if I could read I could do it. I could make a bomb—give me the ingredients and the instructions, and I can do it. Now that I look back at it, I think they were just anxious to get somebody very cheap at that time, and that she would be able to teach me, to mold me, you know, into the way that she wanted.

I was very lonely. There I was, in what was considered an elaborate house compared to what I had been used to. I had a very small room down the basement, and I had never been cooped up like that before, and never lived with white people before. And it was just—I cried about it at night, wanting to go back to what I considered was an awful sort of life in the South. But that was for about a week. You can get used to some things.

I remember the first meatloaf I made. I tried to be very jazzy, and I put meringue on it. It looked beautiful, but it was horrible, absolutely horrible. I don't know what made me think of it—I think I had some egg whites from something, and I said, "Gee, that would be pretty!" I think maybe I had visualized seeing potatoes on top of a meatloaf—you know, mashed potatoes, whipped and browned. But I did the meringue thing. It's really funny because people try not to hurt your feelings—and I know they wanted to throw that crap in the garbage. I couldn't eat it, and they lied and said how nice and good it was—but they never asked me to make a meatloaf again.

The baby girl was a horror. I was brought up under very strict discipline—and to see someone that yelled and shouted at their parents was just something that took some getting used to. In my home you got bashed across the mouth if you ever talked back or anything. I knew what vantage point to talk back—I'd be across the room, or outside, or someplace where I wouldn't be caught. But these kids were really out of control. And I never pretended to try to put them into control—if that's the way that they raised their family, so be it.

I don't think they were bad people—they were the typical kind of family that a young black person would get contact with when they came from the South. I'm saying that now because of the stories I have heard from other people. Of course, I thought that they were very unique at that time. One of things she did—I was making fifteen dollars a week and she said, "I'll save it for you." Not knowing any better, this was great for me. I worked like maybe a month without seeing my money, and then I said, "I'll take my money," and we had a whole discussion about what she owed me. I remember when I first started for her she said not to get acquainted with the other black women who work in the neighborhood because they were not really good people. Of course, they would have said to me, "You're crazy! You're working for fifteen dollars and not taking your pay."

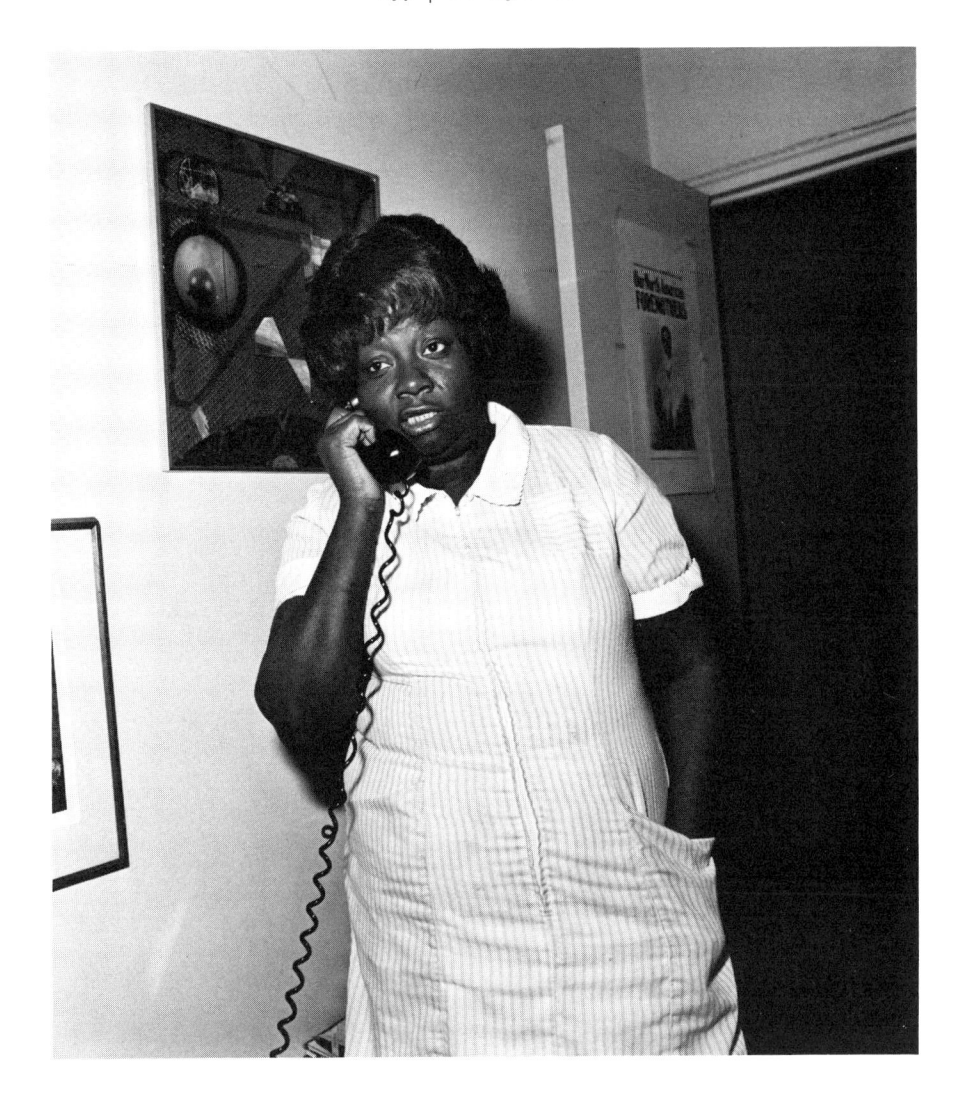

The next job—I left the frying pan and went into the fire. This woman worked the living shit out of me, but she taught me how to clean. Let me tell you—when you finished a day there, you were tired. She had the same strange thing with the money—"I'll save your money for you." When I finally asked for my money, there was confusion as to what I was really owed. It came to the part where I said, "You give me my money or you'll be sorry." You can't even call what she did a paternalistic thing—then she would have kept good records and known how much she owed me.

At that point I was beginning to think that housework was one of the worst things you could do. People sort of looked down on you in your own community if you said that's what you did. Older people used to call it "being in service." I heard that expression just a couple of weeks ago, and I was shocked to still hear it—"in service!" But it was the only thing that I—I didn't have experience in anything else.

Then I began to have—you know, whenever I got tired of a job, I'd just walk away from it. It's the very things that I tell some of our women *not* to do today. If there's something that's wrong, I should be able to talk to you about it. But at the time I wasn't that self-confident, and rather than hurt somebody's feelings and say, "Gee, you were nasty," I'd just pack my little bag and leave, and not even say I was going. Just never show up. Maybe I was scared, probably was—but I think a lot of the time I wasn't scared, it's just that I never liked to hurt people's feelings. I'm much more sure of myself now—I can yell at you and get really mad, but it's just not my style and I prefer not to do it. I dislike anybody yelling at me. Sit down, discuss anything, and I'll listen to you—but if you raise your voice, I won't.

No matter how I felt about my job, I read a lot in my spare time—Nancy Drew books, the Bobbsey Twins, I just read a lot. One thing we were taught in school is to read a paper a day—so I'm one of these freaky people that if I don't have the *Times* and the *News* or some paper, I know I missed something that went on in this world. You should read a paper a day. I got this habit, the first thing I do is see who died. I learned a lot from that because only people who were somebody get in the paper when they die. Like yesterday—a guy who taught at the New School. He was eighty-one years old and he grew up in Germany—he must have been a very interesting person.

I couldn't go back through each job, but I got my biggest education working for a family in Scarsdale. I was still lying about my age, and I think I had upped it a hell of a lot—but actually, I was maybe three or four years older than the oldest child in the house. The father there was a very hard-working man—no inherited money, really worked hard and made a lot of money. He had a thing that you always had to be the boss—and he taught his children this. The daughter wanted to be a nurse, and he said, "Be a doctor—always be the boss!" And I remember that when Jeff reached the age of eighteen, they gave him a million dollars—no strings attached, no trust fund, a million dollars. His mother wrote a note to him and said, "You're very fortunate to have this. Try and take it and help other people because not many people have the opportunity to have this amount of money." He was always a level-headed young man, but that whole family was very weird cause they were always into control.

There were so many things that I predicted. I said, "That old man is gonna push these kids to be what he wants them to be." Jeff bought the local paper, and I said, "Ah, maybe he's getting ready to run for political office." Sure enough, he did. He didn't start off for district leader or assemblyman—he started off for congressman, at twenty something. The scary part is that he almost won because they had the money and the newspaper. That was a very interesting thing for me to watch because I had been a part—I had been involved in that family. I was learning how America works and really not liking what I saw.

That was in the sixties, and I think it was at that point that I began to be politically aware. It was during the time of the civil rights movement, and then you knew exactly where you stood. You knew whether people really cared, or whether it was lip service. One of my biggest educations was when Mrs. Tyree planned a party on the day of the march on Washington. I had to do the party at their country home in Millbrook—oh, how well I remember that! I was just grouchy, really grouchy all day long, because I knew that I was supposed to be in Washington. I would have gone—no doubt about it. The anger that I had that day was really something. I kept the television blaring up all day, and no one dared say anything out of the way to me—you know you just don't fool with somebody when they're in a bad mood. I think she had sixteen people for dinner, and Dr. Monroe said very loud, "I wonder what *they* want?"—"they" meaning black folks—"What *they* need is an education." And I was livid. Normally, I just did the cooking and preparing of the trays, and Kate, an Irish woman, came in and served. So I said, "Katey, let me pass the vegetables. You pour the wine and I will pass the vegetables." It was green beans—and I went out of sequence and went to Dr. Monroe first, and I dumped the beans in his lap. I said, "Gee, I am so sorry. Gee, I really have to be educated as to how to serve beans." And then I left, but they knew, you know.

I had another incident like that when I first came to work here. The Mertons were having a party. Mrs. Merton was in another room setting up the stuff for a slide show, and I was busy going around cleaning up. My husband had come up for the slide show, and he was in there with the guests. Well, God knows you can look at me and tell that I'm black, but with Ken you kind of wonder. He's been accused of being Jewish, Arab, everything—because he's part Irish, part Indian, and part black. Well, he was in there, and this guy started talking about Brazil nuts, calling them "nigger toes." He said it about three times. Ken very seldom gets angry, but when he gets angry, he really gets angry—and it's kind of dangerous because I think you should not let yourself get that way. He said to me, "All he has to do is say that one more time, and he will know what a nigger toe is because I'm gonna kick him in the ass!"

I hustled Ken downstairs and said, "Okay Ken, don't break up the party. I'll take care of it." So the next morning I said to Mrs. Merton, "I have something to discuss with you."

She said, "Yes?"

"About your party last night."

She said, "Wasn't it a marvelous party?"

I said, "No!"

"What do you mean 'no'?"

"Well, one of your guests was making derogatory remarks, and Kenneth almost broke up your party. I just wanted you to know how close you came to it. This man referred to Brazil nuts as 'nigger toes.'"

She was obviously shocked at the whole thing. She said, "I want you to know that that person will never be welcome in this house again." And she wrote Kenneth a note and apologized. And that person has not been back here—and no Brazil nuts have crossed this house since then. She's been very selective, very selective—shelled cashews from then on. We kind of laugh about it now, but yet she does not take a chance on it.

I met Ken when I was working for the Tyrees. Ken went to their church; he didn't go to the black church. I went to church with the Tyrees one Sunday, and he was the only black person in the choir. Actually, I wasn't so sure he was black—I thought he was a little darker than the rest of the people. I found out afterwards, because I asked my friend Evelyn and she said, "Oh, I'll introduce you." So she had a party at her house, and that's how we met. Ken and I dated for three years—I really had no intention of getting married; it wasn't part of my whole thing. But then we got engaged, and I think Mrs. Tyree was afraid of the closeness that Ken and I had developed. Ken and I started making plans, and she says, "Oh, why don't you wait till such-and-such a time, because we would like to give you a wedding." I agreed, and it was a mistake. They always thought that they could do anything with money. Whenever I got very angry about something it was always, "Here's a new dress." But I had worked for three and a half years, close to four years with her, without a vacation. Then it dawned on me, "Hell, I haven't had a vacation! What is this?"

She said, "Go anyplace in the world. We'll pay for it."

But that was not the point—there was no job description at all. You just did what had to be done and sort of went along with what the family needed. If you don't have a contract as to what is to be done, you certainly can get tied up in the family system. So one night we had this one big argument, and she began yelling, so I just left. And a few months later, I married Ken.

Like I said, I had no intention of getting married. I just had not seen many good marriages and didn't want to get involved. I've been very, very lucky, and I think it's something you have to work at. Let me tell you—it was not easy waking up one morning, sharing a bed, a room, a bathroom with somebody when you're used to being alone. That was really a shock! Kenneth was more used to being alone than me, and he valued his aloneness. But all of a sudden, I had something that was mine—another person. It was really funny—this is something we laugh about—because I followed him around all the time, and I didn't realize I was doing it. If he would go from one room to the other, I would follow him. If he went to the bathroom, I would stand outside the door and talk. Finally, one day he said, "I can't stand it! Stop following me! Everyplace I go, you're there!" Then we adjusted our lives.

I came here to the Mertons after Ken and I put an ad in the *New York Times*. We said that we wanted to live in, but the husband was not to work in the home. Ken wanted to go to school—we'd discussed it. Mrs. Merton called me, and we made a date to see each other one evening. My first impression of her was very good. You know, it's classic with people—they must call household workers by their first name. And when she came to meet us at the door she said, "Oh, Mr. and Mrs. Reed, it's so good to see you!" It was so genuine—it's something you don't get so often. We talked to each other about our likes and dislikes, and then she said, "You know, it's awful late for you to have to drive all the way back to Poughkeepsie. The beds are changed in the guest room, if you'd like to stay. And what would you like for breakfast in the morning?" She was really a comedienne! But we still not had made up our minds to take the job. We went back to Poughkeepsie, and two days later we received a telegram from her—it just said HELP! So I took the job. I certainly never regretted it. I like the Mertons, and I adore Dorothy. She's fifty-four and works here three days a week. It's been a marvelous relationship working with her. I love her family, and we call each other every day.

What got me involved in politics—Mrs. Merton always believed that you should be involved in something. She was delighted if you were involved in anything—later, she'd reschedule things so I could go to meetings. So in 1971 I read in the *Amsterdam News* that Edith Barksdale Sloan and other representatives from the National Committee on Household Employment were going to be at some church in Harlem. At the time, I felt very uplifted and glad that there was an organization doing something about the plight of household workers. Josephine Hewlitt really impressed me because she had been a household worker herself, and I could really identify with her. Now, as I look back on the organization, the emphasis at that time was on better educating household workers, not about raising the work benefits of household workers—they wanted to create training programs to have somebody who could better clean a home, better take messages. They swear this wasn't their intention, but this is my perception of it now. I believe in training programs, I think they're necessary—but there has to be a real emphasis put on the employers, because until they get their heads together we're gonna face the same old things.

Later, I went to another meeting. There were only about six women, and they made me the financial secretary—not knowing a damn thing about me, but they just needed people to do things. I came up with this idea of having a luncheon. I was idealistic at that time. My belief was—all you had to do was get to people, and people would do the thing that was right. All they had to do is know that household workers weren't treated right. I started to put together this meeting. I'm not very good at a lot of other things, but I seem to have an expertise at getting people together. I said, "Let's have it at a church someplace—you can get more people to come to church. And let's have it at a place where white folks won't be afraid to come, so we can have a dialogue between the employer and employee." We opted for Riverside Church because it was the church that I attended, and they gave us the assembly hall free. We got them to cater a luncheon for three dollars a person, and we charged five dollars so we could have some money in the treasury.

All of us was to sell tickets to our employers—so we were gonna have the same amount of employers there as employees. And we just talked it up, you know. I think black women are very good at selling tickets. Listen, I could go out on the street there and sell anybody—they'd buy it just to get me off their back. As a drawing card we had Eleanor Holmes Norton as the keynote speaker. She was the director of Human Rights and had just finished a study on household employment. We sold a hundred and eighty tickets, and Mrs. Merton was the only employer that showed up. We all said, "The hell with the employer! If this is the way they feel, we'll do it ourselves."

After that I began to get involved with other organizations to be able to help my own organization. You have to be involved in a lot of other things in order to ascertain your own goals. It was definitely an education for me. I was happy to be involved with the feminist groups. Before even knowing the word, I had always, in a sense, been a feminist. That was just me, just the way I was. I would never think of being put down as a woman and thinking that I am some sort of—somebody's object, you know—that I *belong* to Ken. It's just never been that way. So I was happy to be involved with the National Black Feminist Organization, with helping to found that organization. And then I worked with the Manhattan Women's Political Caucus, an interracial group.

One of the things that I encountered when I first began being involved with some of the feminist groups was that they acted like their attitude about housework was the meaning it had to have. It was something they had to get their heads together on. I remember that the Household Technicians were doing a party for Gloria Steinem, over on the West Side in an environmental apartment—really something, really weird. The place had no door on anything, not even the bathroom—but there were mirrors so you could see someone coming. They couldn't see you, so you had to yell, "I'm in here!" We were paid quite well, a professional fee, to cater that party. We had on black uniforms, and it freaked out some of the feminist women there. They could not deal with it. They said, "Poor maids—they got maids here, we're leaving."

I remember having to get up and say to them, "Hold it, cool it! First of all, I don't like you to think we're *maids*—we are household technicians; we've experienced; we are professionals. And we're being paid—that's very important. We need money, we're being paid, and we're going to be respected—so you have to get it out of your head that this is a demeaning job. If you don't want to do it, I'm glad that you don't want to, because we will gladly do it for you—but for a salary, and with respect; the same as other people get—as a job, as a profession." Most of my efforts have been getting that into people's heads. And I explained to them that the uniform is the uniform of my profession. It's just like a doctor wearing his white coat. I think you feel kind of uncomfortable if you go into a lab and the doctor doesn't have that white coat on—you don't think of him being the doctor. It's just the simple thing of a uniform, but it's there. And I said, "So I choose to wear my uniform. I'm not gonna ruin my clothes—you may spill something on me."

There was a positive reaction. I think what my speech did was relieve people of their guilt feeling that, "Oh, gee, now I don't have to feel guilty. She's feeling okay about it, so now I don't have to feel guilty." I think that's what it was.

We call our group the Household Technicians of America because we wanted to get away from *servant, maid,* and *domestic*. When I think of *domestic*, I immediately think of a very tame animal—a cat or a dog or something. I am not a tame person, I am not a domesticated person. And I don't even know how it came that *domestic* is related to household workers. Maybe I should look it up in the dictionary. *Servant* to me goes back to the days of slavery. That's what they called the people who worked in their homes—their *servants*—and that is what they were. A *servant* is anybody who waits on you. That's why I don't like the word. *Maid* just seems like a put-down to me. *Maid* to me seems like a possession—like, "This is my *maid*."

With Mrs. Merton, she always introduced me as her friend. Ken and myself met them at theater one night, and Mrs. Merton was with these friends who were obviously racists. She said, "Let me introduce you—these are my friends, the Taylors and the Reeds."

This Mrs. Taylor says, "Don't they work for you, Julie?"

She said, "Yes."

Mrs. Taylor would have been happier if Mrs. Merton had said, "These are my maids."

Girl falls under the same category. They still use it. But *help,* I really have no problems with that, because that's what you're doing—you are helping someone. I don't know whether I'd like to be referred to constantly as *the help* in the house, but it does not bother me as much as *maid, servant,* and *girl*. I have a thing that—you ask me how I would like to be addressed, and I will ask you how you would like to be addressed. You know, it's just automatic where women are referred to by their first names, and men are referred to as Mr. Big Shit. I have no problem with *household worker,* because that's exactly what we are—we work in households.

Here are the things we think household workers are entitled to. Definitely health benefits—hospitalization, very good medical coverage. Of course, I believe in the National Health Plan, but we don't have it yet. There should be a retirement plan too. When people try to save money and don't pay social security, it hurts us. And you know what ultimately happens—a person working off the books is the same person that is gonna eventually end up on the welfare dollar. We should have some kind of pension plan that we could look forward to, that we could contribute to.

You have that plus your medical coverage and you can live. I just think that our well-being should no longer be subject to the whims of people—you know, whether a person's good or bad. We want legislation, a set of guidelines you have to go by.

All this may mean a restructuring of the whole field of household employment. Maybe it means that each family in that apartment building over there doesn't need to have someone living in their home. Maybe there should be a cooperative run by household workers—and rather than call an employment agency, you have an operation running right in that building. It would be less personal, but the work would be done. See, another thing that I want to get away from is that household workers have been conditioned to believe that living in is a fringe benefit. It is not—it's a condition of the job. The majority of women would prefer not to live in, because even if they do live in they rent rooms someplace that they're responsible for. It's not a fringe benefit for us, but for the person who is the employer. Even the way it's advertised—"Live in: room and board plus salary." Like that is a benefit. I think it has to be said enough so that people understand—it is not a benefit! Maybe it was a benefit when I first came North—but a lot of the younger women had rooms, and I subsequently got a room. You need something that's your own. I remember, Mr. Tyree used to try to tell me how great it was to live in Scarsdale. I said, "Nothing is so hot about Scarsdale. My friends don't live here. I have to go out of Scarsdale to see my friends, where maybe you can go next door."

When I think of people who've supported us, the first name that comes up is Gloria Steinem. What Gloria has done is not just the whole media thing. She does many things for us—and what I like is that she is accessible without the whole fanfare. She was the person who has been most consistent—really putting her money and her actions where her mouth is, just constantly doing it and not really seeking publicity for it. I've known her to go down to Washington for a luncheon and to rush back here later on for a meeting of ours that she could have obviously gotten out of. And at her own expense, not ours. You can call on her and get action. One time I said, "Gloria, we gotta have a superstar for this fund-raising, and you're the superstar, and you've got to wear this apron." Gloria put on the apron and did it. About the apron—we had a fund-raising for the National Committee, and we developed the idea of honoring the household workers by getting famous guests to serve the workers. And we got Gloria; Mary Anne Krupsak, who's the lieutenant governor; Werner Krumowski, who heads the Human Rights Commission; Lenny Proberman; and Esther Rolle, who starred as Florida in the "Maude" series. They all did it, they put on aprons and passed the trays around. Mary Anne and Lenny Proberman commented that the moment they had a tray in their hands they became invisible—that people didn't know what to say to them. Here was the lieutenant governor walking around with a tray, and the guests were doing the obvious thing—not even looking. It was really incredible!

Mary Anne Krupsak has helped in many ways. Besides giving money, she worked very hard on the passage of our bill in Albany, even though it was Seymour Posner's bill. I spent many a day in Albany, and as lieutenant governor she runs the Senate. She'd come off the Senate floor and bring the person who was the opposition, and we'd sit down and talk about it. The bill was to give collective-bargaining rights to household workers, and she played a very important part in there because she had the inside track. You see, it's very easy to just put a bill out and say that you're working for it—which makes me kind of annoyed with Seymour Posner. Of course, he would propose that kind of bill—his constituency is mainly black and Puerto Rican, and he would have to do something to appeal to that. If the bill doesn't pass, it doesn't hurt him because he can say at least it was his bill. And he never consulted household workers in advance to see if this is what they wanted. This was his baby, you know. And the thing was, he said, "Well, my mother was a household worker."

I say, "Sy, don't pull that one on me, because you're not black. Cut the crap!"

He said, "Well, she was a practical nurse, but that was just a household worker anyhow. She had to do this, and she died doing this."

And I said, "Sy, all sympathy to your mother—she was still a white woman, and she had a better chance than a black woman."

Then he said I was being a racist.

Another person who has been very helpful is Esther Peterson. She works for Giant Food Products—head of the consumer division—but she's also head of Consumer Affairs for the United States government. She's an older woman who's been around consumerism all her life. She was one of the original founders of the National Committee, and I think she's shown a great interest in having people trained for the whole thing.

Another person who did a lot was Anna Halstead—President Roosevelt's daughter. Until she died, she was very close to the committee. There've been a host of people who have been really, really helpful—but if I had to say who has been the most helpful person to me personally, I would have to say—and this may sound a little bit corny—but it would have to be Kenneth. He moans and groans and types up stuff for me. He sort of takes the pressure off. He says everything is all right when I know damn well it isn't. And he has just been consistently—"Do what you feel you have to do. Don't feel that you have to be under any kind of pressure."

On our mailing list—the people who expressed an interest, and who at one time or another became part of the organizational structure—are twenty-five thousand people across the country. In New York it fluctuates between five different groups, from two hundred and fifty to seven hundred. You are lucky if you can get fifteen active women for a meeting. For instance, Eva McQuay is having a block party—you'll get some people who will be very interested, and some who won't come.

Right now I'm disappointed because the National Committee on Household Employment should have attained a lot more than it has. I look back at its history, and it's to the point now where I feel personally that people are more interested in keeping jobs and getting funding than in getting things done. The National Committee is having a conference in October, which is very distracting to me. I think maybe this is the year that we should not have a conference, because people can't afford it. Maybe we should encourage the local organizations to have conferences to get together in their own communities. I mean, there are different ways of doing it than by what's down in the book, or by what people say is the way that you do it. You can find your own way—you have to. We learn from the experiences of each other, but I hear the same things, conference after conference. I mean, we could meet and think up catchy terms. I'm sure that's what all organizations do—anything to appeal to the media—but I think what I'm gonna be about is the nuts and bolts of getting something done. How do you get the most for what you have? How do you get people motivated? I think we have to think about defining our own goals and not imitating others.

In my reading I discovered we are at a point in our history household workers were at in 1918. They were doing the same thing then. I was amazed. I thought, "Gee, I developed this unique idea." And then I find out that in 1918 somebody had the same unique idea, and it hadn't worked. We haven't progressed. Okay, we got a little piece—we got a bill passed in Albany—but I still feel very strongly that there has to be more laws on the book, that we have to be in the main stream of labor. Labor has to recognize us as a force. And how do you do that? Maybe it's developing a union of our own. Some unions want us to join with them, but who says we have to belong to George Meany, who doesn't give a shit. I mean, how well does George Meany pay the person who works in his home?

In the last few years, if a journalist wanted to know anything about household work, they'd go to Carolyn Reed. I wanna get away from the media image of being the super household worker. I'm gonna take a year and sort of, as people say, "get my shit together." Our group devoted too much time to supporting other groups, and that's basically my fault— not really knowing how to control my time, and wanting to become involved in so much. There are people out there who can do it for awhile— and I want to let them do it, and do it their way. Sometimes you feel that you can be a hindrance. When you have been identified as the person who knows all about it, people feel that they can't express themselves because you're gonna be around sort of looking over their shoulder. You should step back—not to let it regress, but to build it. I'd love to let someone come out of the movement and overshadow me—it would be helpful. And then I'd want that person to give other people a chance to do it too. I never want things to be so centered around an individual, but I see some people who won't let go—the Roy Wilkins complex. I'm sure to this day he did not want to retire. They really forced him to it. I don't think you should have to be forced into something like that.

I'll tell you one last thing about household work. Dorothy Pittman, who started the West Side Day Care centers, told me this story one time when we were talking about this whole thing of people saying, "I want you to feel a part of the family—this is your home." When Dorothy came up from the South to live, this woman did the whole act on her—"This is your home, the house is yours." Dorothy invited her boyfriend for dinner—he rings the doorbell, comes in the front door, and sits down in the living room. Dorothy had gotten pork chops for dinner that night—happens to be an orthodox Jewish family. She fried her pork chops and everything. She said she noticed that the woman looked very strange, you know. She didn't say anything, and after the guy left she said, "You know, Dorothy, I'd like to talk to you. Now it's okay for your friends to come here, but you should entertain them in your own room."

Dorothy told her, "Now you said that I should treat this as my home, and back home I was never allowed to take boys in my bedroom."

The thing is that you're *not* a part of the family—you are an employee. Yes, there is no way that you cannot get involved in family life. I get involved with what goes on in the lives of the Mertons by virtue that I am here. You can't help a certain amount of involvement—but I'm still not a Merton; I'm still not a part of that family. I want us to get away from the paternalistic thing and get it on a keel where it's a profession. This is what I do as a profession; I am proud to do this as a profession, and I'm being paid for it—just stop all the crap!